A SPIRITUAL PRIMER

THE GREAT AWAKENING

LINDA DILLON

The Great Awakening: A Spiritual Primer

© 2012 by Linda Dillon

All rights reserved

Dedication

This book is dedicated to the Council of Love, and to every Lightworker on the planet.

Spread the good news – hope reigns and Love wins.

Table of Contents

Chapter 3 The Thirteenth Octave Blessings & Virtues 83

Chapter 4 The Gift of the Violet Flame 95

Chapter 5 Universal Mother Mary's Gift of the Blue Diamond 115

Blessings and Gratitudes

Where do I begin with my gratitude and heartfelt thank-yous? This book is the culmination of more than twenty years of working with the Council of Love. The Great Awakening is my life's work, and although it is the beginning not the end, it marks a completion for me in many ways.

The danger in creating acknowledgements is forgetting someone or making them feel that somehow their contribution was underrated. That is simply not possible here. I have so much to be grateful for. The support I have received for many years has been phenomenal. This is the abbreviated version so if you don't see your name look up and see it written in the heavens. Each of you has graced my journey in loving insightful ways.

I begin by my acknowledgements with my family – the technical, editing, inspirational, mind provoking, soul-searching, late-night conversations, laughter and tears have support me in every way. I thank my beloved, Isaac, for his unwavering faith in his "angel talker." I thank him for anchoring me and for encouraging me to fly as high and as often as need be. There is a special place in my heart for my siblings who have not only seen me through this incredible and sometimes incomprehensible journey of spirit. My sisters, Suzanne and Debay, are my bedrock of sanity and of love. They are always there for me through thick and thin, fat and skinny, and always reminded me that all that really counts is love, and making time for each other no matter what. My brother, Joe, is my touchstone, a role model of the balance between being grounded and leading the spiritual life. My brother, Pat, shows me that although the path is sometimes rocky and you don't know what lies ahead, you just keep going, in trust and with a smile. My cousin, Patricia, is my anchor, helpmate and private booster club in this project and my life. My nieces, Linda and Kara, and my nephew, Michael, are my inspiration, reminding me why I do this – they are the next generation and they get it!

There is a small legion of friends whom I know as soul family who support me in being and becoming who I am. There have been times when the encouragement and support has been emotional, spiritual and even financial. They never let me give up and continue to remind me that I am here for a purpose and that means something in the bigger picture. My love to my first supporters and co-creators, Lisa Nouvelle and Michael Callas, Judy Barron and Maggi Casteel, Shawn Hull and June McGregor. Thank you to my old friends and fellow travelers Janet Zimmer and Joe Vasile – thanks for the memories, the laughter and courage. A special thank you also to Joanna Brock, Rosy Lucky, and Judy Tozzi.

I don't know if I would still be here without my soul sisters Pam Barron, Mary Valanzano, Roz Lett, Marianne Baer, Suzanne Wendelken, and Carol Bakunas. They prop me up, reinforce me when I go through my questioning and soul-searching. They remind me I'm not crazy and yes this is all worth it – we are changing the world, one person at a time. Which brings me to Taka, my soul brother and muse, my side-kick and trusted friend. He always understands the bigger picture and what the Council has in store.

Heartfelt thank you also go to my to my star sisters, Nishia Klein and Dashell Anne Kronen, for expanding my understanding and love for our star brothers and sisters; and to Elizabeth Patric for sharing the magic of the kingdoms, especially the flowers and the fairies.

The list could be endless for there are many of you I love and who are so generous with your energy and support. I want to say a special thank you to my Council of Love family who has traveled with me for so long – in Sedona, Michigan, New York, Florida, Colorado, California and Arizona. A final thank you for my two best angel friends, Ruth and Azurel. You always had my back and you still hold my heart. You are sorely missed, and your visits are greatly appreciated.

My final heartfelt thank you is to the Council of Love. Little did I know or even begin to comprehend the shift that would occur in my life the day I first heard "Welcome from the Council of Love." I am eternally grateful and blessed. Thank you for helping me remember who I am and why I came. I wouldn't change it for the world.

Preface

On the night of December 27, 1984, I died. The drive home was brutal. But as the saying goes "you ain't seen nothing yet." Pulling onto our exit, we hit black ice. In those frozen moments we flew up one side of a hill and bounced ass-over-tea-kettle-down. That's when I left my body and found myself standing in a cold winter night's sky with my guardian angel Nathaniel.

What was weirder – standing in thin air, or being with an angel? Angel, hands down. I felt no pain, just the warm connection that somehow I had always known. Gently, Nathaniel told me it was time to make a decision to stay or return home – to die. It wasn't a high drama moment; it was calm, peaceful, just a choice. I knew very clearly that I had not completed the mission or reason I chose to be born. I didn't know what that reason was, but I knew beyond a doubt that I hadn't done it yet. And so, I chose to live.

The recovery was long and painful – it was a time before much was understood about crushed bodies and closed head injuries. But what happened during those years of recovery is the beginning of the story. I had always had a strong spiritual life and connection with the universe but I kept it in what I believed was proper perspective. I avidly pursued a career that I loved in human services. I was helping people and communities with issues that need addressing for the disenfranchised, disabled and under-privileged. I was doing good work. Work that obviously laid the foundation for what was to come but miles away from what became my soul/sole journey.

In an effort to stay sane, and relieve pain, it was suggested that I try meditating. While I had done deep prayer work and taken a little yoga, meditating was a foreign concept to me. However, lying in bed and having no other alternatives to deal with the pain I began. I relaxed, began with a little prayer and asked for help. Immediately a huge golden orb appeared in my mind's eye and hovered over me, moving from my head down my body to my feet and back again. The process was repeated several times. Then an orb of the most beautiful rich emerald green I have ever seen appeared and repeated the same process. I felt warm, relaxed and the pain was reduced. Wow – maybe there's something to this meditation stuff.

After several days, I was feeling remarkably better, emotionally and physically but I was also curious as all get out – what was going on? So one morning when the golden orb appeared on schedule I asked –"Who are you?" I don't know why but I definitely knew it was a who. A booming voice answered "I am Gabriel, Lily of Love, Trumpet of Truth." I repeated the process with the emerald orb and received a more modest reply "I am James, Apostle of our Lord Jesus Christ, Savior, Son of God." Now I knew that I had crossed the line from depression and discouragement to being absolutely off my rocker. But because I kept feeling better I ignored common sense and kept going.

After a couple of weeks of this morning routine I was compelled to get up, go to my kitchen table, get pen and paper and start writing. You could say I felt I was in an altered state. After making squiggles and circles on the paper my hand began to move of its own volition and the words appeared Welcome to the Council of Love. Immediately I asked who they were and the answer they gave is the answer I relate to this day:

"The Council of Love is God's sacred alliance composed of angels, Archangels, enlightened saints, the Apostles, the Unified Forces of the Outer Galaxies, and the Ascended Masters. The purpose of the Council is the transmission of the Divine Radiance and Love into the hearts of all beings who wish to align and receive. The Council are messengers of the One and the message is Love. The primary messenger for the Council is Archangel Gabriel, Lily of Love and Trumpet of Truth."

As if this wasn't enough for one lifetime when I asked what

they wanted with me Gabriel's answer was they wanted to talk and teach and prepare humanity for the Shift. I had no idea what the Shift was – talking to non-physical beings was enough without them telling me that I was to be their messenger to help the world prepare for the Shift. Nevertheless, they began to talk about the Shift – and while the primary speakers were Archangel Gabriel and the Apostle James they were regularly joined by others of the heavenly realm particularly Archangel Michael, Jesus and Mother Mary.

The Council told me that the Shift was a shift for Earth and humanity from the third dimension of duality to the seventh dimension of Christ Consciousness. Part of this Shift would involve a tilt in the Earth's axis south by southwest, by seven-point-three degrees which would result in massive destruction and that about three percent of the world's population would survive. It would require great preparation and re-location of many if they were to survive. It was explained not only as a cleansing of Earth's surface because of the devastation that had occurred on Gaia but the unfoldment of Divine Plan. The decision was Gaia's to wipe her face clean and begin again with the original plan of the Universal Mother which was for Earth to be a planet of Love – a place where angels could come and play and experience physicality, the opportunity to experience Love and joy in form.

Needless to say this information weighed heavily on me – if I believed (and I did) what I was being told, then massive disaster was coming in future years and I was to be a modern day Noah. If it wasn't true, then I had clearly lost my mind. Now in many ways I already felt that I had lost my life with injuries and being stuck in "recovery" but this was too much. Talk about a no-win situation. But at the same time a miraculous door had opened for me. The connection to these beings was so strong, so loving, so healing and so real. I did not feel isolated or alone, I felt loved, cherished and supported, as if they knew the magnitude of what they were telling and asking of me. I did not want to let go of this connection.

One morning as I sat at the kitchen table with my unseen

friends, they communicated a little and then wrote they would not write any more. I was devastated. Finally I had this incredible connection and it was being taken away. The sense of loss was overwhelming. I staggered back into my bedroom and pulled the covers over my head and stayed there in deep dark depression for days.

This link had been so sweet, so fulfilling, that I decided I was not above begging. So once again, I returned to my kitchen table and the morning ritual, anxious, fearful, and distraught – what kind of loving beings would do this to me – had I not suffered enough? Was I not strong or willing or ready enough to take on the role they had proposed for me? As I sat there feeling this despair the pen started moving once again – first circles like always then the always consistent greeting "welcome from the Council of Love." Then they went to the place on the page where I had ended my last transmission and finished the sentence "we will not write any more because we wish to speak through you."

My heart leapt for joy – I wasn't on the outs after all! And so began my training as a full channel for the Council of Love. This incredible group of enlightened beings have led me every step of the way for almost thirty years. There have been victories, struggles, personal challenges but the essence has always remained the same – I am their channel and I am here to help humanity through the Shift. The plan has been modified, clarified and the pieces put in place to assist each of you in this process of Shift, of Ascension, of fulfilling your mission and purpose in the unfoldment of the Mother's Plan.

Introduction

Over the course of the next thirty years the Council kept me very busy. They channeled a series of courses on the essentials of spiritual growth, laying the foundation for our collective Ascension with Gaia. It's amazing and heart-warming when you realize that all the work you've done for years comes neatly together like the pieces of a puzzle. So it is with this book, The Great Awakening, tying together the teaching, gifts and attunements of the Council of Love.

One of the very first things the Council ever spoke to me about – after I vehemently demanded that they identify themselves and their purpose – was The Shift. They were, and always have been crystal clear with me, that a major part of my purpose was to prepare people for the Shift – the inter-dimensional Shift from the third to the fifth and onward to the seventh. For years this is something I kept very low key, choosing and being guided to keep people's eyes and more importantly their hearts on the issues at hand – of anchoring Divine Union, at finding trust and forgiveness – self-worth; joy, co-creation – in a nutshell Love.

In those early days – almost thirty years ago, predictions regarding the Shift were quite dire and I can remember doing a lot of crying in the first six months. But Lightworkers everywhere awoke, and sent healing to each other and to Gaia, and the picture changed. The Council began to shower us with gifts and tools and we surged forward; 11:11 and 12:12 came. People joined together in earnest and meaningful ways – I began to see the light and the wisdom of Universal Mother Mary's Plan of Unfoldment.

Before we leave those early days I would like to talk about Archangel Gabriel or Archangel Gabrielle as she chooses to be known. It took me years to publicly acknowledge that I was channeling Archangel Gabriel. It felt like hubris to even suggest such a thing. But at the same time, since day one, Archangel Gabrielle has been my go-to guide, the spokesbeing for the Council of Love who has shepherded me through this incredible journey.

Initially Gabriel called himself Suzanna Michaela Gabrielle, explaining that the Suzanna is a derivative of suzerain, indicative of leadership; and Michaela was in honoring and respect for Archangel Michael. But this forthright Archangel has always been very insistent that she comes to us in the feminine form. While Archangels are usually considered androgynous, I have found it amazing over the years how many people object or wish to correct my understanding of the feminine nature of Gabrielle. Hence I mention it here before we get started. I end this discussion with a quote from our beloved Archangel: "Child do you really think that they would send a male energy to inform a young Jewish virgin that she was pregnant out of wedlock?" That dear readers is our Gabrielle, she is funny, and direct bilks no argument.

The Council has been clear that all we need to "get home" is Love, trust, forgiveness, unity, connectedness and balance. So what's left do?

The COL uses the analogy of climbing Mount Everest to explain not only our individual journey but also Ascension. All you need to climb Everest is a healthy body, meaning your heart and the full connection to Love. I have not only strenuously objected to but actually found very distasteful those "channelings" that have suggested that in this dimensional transition, in this plan of the renewal of Love on Terra Gaia, some get to go and some are left behind – the underlying insinuation being that some are "not quite ready or there yet." It's far too wheat and chaff for this girl. How could that ever be of Love?

The Council of Love makes it abundantly clear that all are welcome – equally and wholly. Every being, every kingdom, every elemental, every blade of grass is welcome to join with Gaia in this journey as she ascends – she is already well underway. The teachings of the Council have always been practical and applicable to our here and now lives – it has never been about mystery schools or far out esoteric practices. It is accessible and for everyone. But before we go into the particulars of "how to" let's take a brief look at the past twenty-five years of this collective journey; the meaning of the 11:11 and 12:12 portal openings and what our next steps will look like.

Nineteen-eighty-seven marked the beginning of this twenty-five-year Ascension process. This is not to say that the Ascension process began in 1987 – that has been going on for thousands of years, but for our human understanding most of us think and can grapple with a twenty-five-year span. It also marks the beginning of our conscious collective awareness that we were involved in a change process – many have not been aware of exactly what this change fully was about, but few would deny that radical Shift has been in every aspect of our lives in the past couple of decades.

The Harmonic Convergence in 1987 jump-started or activated most starseeds on the planet. Starseeds are humans who have travelled the galaxies and lived on other planets, and even distant galaxies, and who have chosen to reincarnate here on Earth at this juncture for the specific purpose of assisting with this Ascension process and Shift. This awakening, this "dawn of the age of Aquarius" marked the beginning of conscious awareness of massive numbers of people working with the higher realms, inter-dimensional beings, including our star brothers and sisters, and becoming active transmuters. Examples of this awakening include the explosion of energy healing, the widespread acceptance and belief in angels and alternate realities, the migration of many young people to the East, to India and Tibet, in search of enlightenment. These changes were not simply the birth of a counter-culture but the inner knowing that something fundamental was changing. Each of us has consciously and unconsciously been on this Ascension quest for years.

November 11, 1992 marked the opening of the spiritual and inter-dimensional portal known as 11:11. This huge opening marked the beginning of the collective movement into the Love and into the One. It began widespread reports and experiences of inter-dimensional travel and extra-terrestrial contact. In February 1992 the Council gave their first channeled workshop on planetary changes and the Shift – the teaching began in earnest. In June of the same year at a COL workshop, we were guided to send pink to the planet "as this planet spins from the third to the seventh dimension it is essential (if you wish to remain upon her) that you send her this love. In this way you become a magnet, and as the electro-magnetic fields change, you are able to stay grounded upon her face. Otherwise, you will think of self as simply flying off into space when the Shift begins to occur."

On December 12, 1993 there was opening of a second portal; one which came to be known as 12:12 portal. This opening marked the beginning of physical changes both within our DNA and electro-magnetic grid, as well as our esoteric bodies. The theme of 12:12 was and is the challenge and anchoring of balance and joy. One of the things often misunderstood is, these portals did not open and then close or disappear. The 12:12 portal for example is a portal process of twenty years – a portal of Ascension preparation with numerous phases which will conclude at the end of 2020.

When the 12:12 portal opened, the Council described it in this way: "This is a time of great change. The entry into the transition of 12:12 is not a time to be taken lightly. Many have avoided the decision of whether to stay or go, but know that decisions are being made on a soul level. It is a time where it is important to align with your holy decision; it is a time to enter the wholeness of your sacred being and to enter into Joy."

The channeled workshops on joy began in earnest. There was a further opening of the 12:12 portal in 1994, one which marked what the Council termed the time of plenty.

James the Apostle explained it this way: "It is important to understand the octave of 12:12. This octave is the time of Love incarnate on Earth. It is the time when many of the knowing masters return to the planet to teach and show the way of balance. The restoration of balance is necessary for the final journey homeward. One cannot travel lopsided, be it a person or a planet. The gifts of 12:12 are the tools to re-establish balance within thy star pattern, in a collective and planetary sense. Joy, which is necessary for Ascension, is the fuel of thy star. Love is the ignition, creation is the vehicle."

The star pattern reference is to the various aspects of our being – starseed, earth-keeper, destroyer, creator and I AM presence. In other words our galactic self who hails from the stars, that part of ourselves committed to the nurturing of Gaia and her journey through Ascension. The destroyer aspect wields the sword of Archangel Michael, and is capable of cutting through illusion and false paradigms, revealing the truth; and our creator self brings forward that which we desire to experience during our journey on Earth, including the Shift. To anchor this knowing of your various aspects within your physical self, picture yourself back in high school gym class – standing with your arms fully extended in a "V" above your shoulders; legs akimbo. Your right arm extension is your warrior self; your opposite left leg is your creator self. Your left extended arm is your starseed self and your right leg is your earth-keeper self. Your head, especially your crown represents your I AM presence. Now pull and feel each of those energies anchoring in your heart. The integration of each of these aspects equally is important. You will feel these aspects change positions at different times depending on what you are working on. Just allow that re-positioning, be the observer, and pay attention that you are not living in just one aspect.

The symbolism and messages of the 12:12 cannot be overlooked either. In the realm of human experience there are twelve dimensions that can be experienced. Within each of these dimensions are twelve planes of existence – hence the continued reference throughout all cultures to the importance of one hundred forty-four. All of these dimensional realities are open to us. Most of us have emanated from a higher dimension. Think of these twelve dimensions and the twelve planes of existence within the human realm as steps or layers on the golden spiral. Each dimension can also be thought of as an octave – the octave being a spiritual reference to the right tone of being. Prior to 1997 with the gift from the Heart of One of the Thirteenth Octave, all humans could collectively experience without dying was the twelve dimensions or octaves. Both the qualities of the twelve dimensions, and the gifts of the Thirteenth Octave are discussed in detail in Chapter One.

Now, back to the Mount Everest analogy. Yes, all you need is your strong body – the Love. However, it will make your ascent much smoother and easier if you have certain things and your "kit bag" and a Sherpa (the Council) to guide you. The items for the kit bag or your backpack if you want to be au moderne are the things the Council has given us over the past fifteen years, plus the energetic attunements they are channeling and transmitting to your core during the reading of this book and the accompanying meditations. Some are deliciously surprising; others anticipated. These are described briefly below, and in detail in subsequent chapters.

Little did I know as I floated around my swimming pool in the summer of 1996 that I was about to embark upon an incredible journey with the Council of Love – one that would lead all of us in a progression of growth, discovery and Love; a journey that has built soul family, sacred circle and anchored friendships above and below that are dear and enduring through thick and thin. What began as the information and download of the Thirteenth Octave has grown and morphed into a community committed to the process of change and fulfillment of the Mother's promise.

That gift of the Thirteenth Octave was and is enormous. It literally changed not only my world but the lives of everyone who has said yes and stepped forward to join in this state of union. In addition to the initiation and re-connection, the gifts of the Thirteenth Octave have been numerous. Each COL workshop is bestowed with an array of gifts and tools (e.g. Mary's gift of removal, Gabriel's golden infinity, Uriel's silver flame to mention a few) to complete our missions here on Earth with Grace, Love, and Joy.

The annual COL Sedona Gathering became a time when the Council shared with us the agenda for the upcoming year, blessing us with the tools and gifts necessary for going forward on our spiritual journey – and reinforcing us by the strength of coming together in our sacred circle. It is a gathering of soul family and friends who come together year after year to laugh and play and reconnect – it is a chance for everyone to know not only that we're not crazy but that we're not alone.

Through these annual gatherings, the Council has led us through a process of teaching, opening and expanding us. It began with the Thirteenth Octave, went on to accessing the Universal Internet, which taught us how to access the grid and how to use the gifts being bestowed upon us. That class was the beginning of the channeling course. Next came Angel Wings and working with our future selves, the Wingmakers; then Partnerships: Human and Divine, moving us from our sole/soul journey into union and community. These were followed by areas I never dreamt of teaching, but the Council had other ideas – Heart & Healing; Channeling; Creation and Co-Creation; Joy and Wisdom Vision. The list is long but I have a sense that it has only just begun.

When I look at how far we have come as a Lightworker and as a Lightholder community, I am humbled. I also realize that all of this preparation has been leading us to this point so that we may ascend together as one circle of Love.

The gifts and attunements that prepare us for smooth and complete Ascension are the following:

The Thirteenth Octave Process of Divine Union

The miraculous gift of the Thirteenth Octave was first bestowed upon us on December 12, 1997. This process of Divine Union has been shared with thousands of people since that time, and continues to be shared and spread daily.

The ability to join in sacred Divine Union – to go home and unite with the heart of God, without dying has never been available to humanity before. "It is a gift from the heart of One." The benefits of the Thirteenth Octave and of being in that place of union as we journey forward are obvious – we're already there. Another benefit of the Thirteenth Octave process is one that I have talked about for years but few have really heard. When you enter into the Thirteenth Octave your twelve strands of DNA are fully activated and bundled into a Thirteenth single strand.

Archangel Gabrielle puts it this way, "To date, that was all that was truly available to those within your energy grid of twelve planes and twelve existences. This has now changed. God created the next energy plane, the next circle long ago, but it has never been open or available to those in physical form on Earth. That is why it initially will be difficult for some to understand and accept. Those in a state of advanced knowing, those who through their daily ritual of joining with the Divine will be the least resistive. They have always known that there was much more beyond the veil, they have always prayed that they would enter the next phase alive, conscious and ready."

The Thirteen Blessings and Virtues

The anchoring of the thirteen Blessing and Virtues are part of the initiation into the Thirteenth Octave. They are incredible and beautiful – and often overlooked. When I began questioning the inclusion of this in our Ascension process Archangel Gabrielle in all her might and glory became very insistent. With Sanat Kumara, keeper of Universal Law and Planetary Logos at her side, I didn't stand a chance.

Archangel Gabrielle clarified: "Child you are seeing the disillusion of the old paradigms of Earth; the elimination of lack, limitation, control, greed, death, destruction, disease – but what would you have replace this? What is the new foundation upon which Nova Earth is built? It is the thirteen Blessings and Virtues that we gifted you so long ago. This is the core of everything you will value and bring forth in the new reality. This is the foundation of what you create and co-create with us. If the virtues are not an inherent part of your being how do you then translate into form as you build the new institutions, systems, communities, and cultures of Nova Earth?"

James the Apostle explained it this way: "Know that when we speak of the concept of blessings and virtues that the terms are interchangeable. If one has a virtue it is indeed a blessing not only to the individual but to the whole. While there are many, many blessings and virtues, which are available throughout the Universe, we speak this day of the core virtues necessary to go forward without blockages or debris. It allows one to maintain a state of wholeness. This grouping of blessings and virtues is intended to equip you with those qualities necessary to complete your mission of service to others. Each carries a distinct vibration that will become irrevocably a part of your being during the initiation process."

Gift of the Violet Flame of St. Germaine

St. Germaine is the Master of the Violet Flame, the Healing Temple of the Violet Flame and the I AM Presence. In 2001, St. Germaine began extending initiation into his sacred temple, citing that he required "an armada of healers to assist in the healing and transformation of Gaia and humanity, and, the creation of Nova Earth."

As this beloved Master teaches us, the purpose of healing, connecting and anchoring in the I AM presence is to transmute and connect – to help transform. "Together, hand in hand, in healing heart, we will create Nova Earth, the place where none is left in desolation of darkness believing they are unloved."

The Initiation into the Violet Flame was given once again via a special broadcast on Sept. 17, 2011. If you missed it you can still go to the front page of the COL website and play it and receive the initiation. The link is www.counciloflove.com.

Universal Mother Mary's Gift of the Blue Diamond

This is the gift of Mother Mary's very essence, originally gifted in 2002 and renewed regularly ever since that momentous time. The Blue Diamond is not something from her – it is her – her love, her nurturing, her healing transmitted directly into your heart and core. It is our anchoring of the Divine Feminine within our beings, including our physical bodies.

Our sacred Divine Mother explains it this way "I gave you my essence, my very core of Blue Diamond that you would be filled with Mother's Love but also with my power, with my nurturing, with my knowledge, with my wisdom, with my strength, with my endurance, with my patience. All of this is part and parcel now not only of who I am but of who you are. It was not a selective gift. Each of you on Earth is continually infused with my essence of Blue Diamond. And I will do this until you return home and far after if you wish."

Mother Mary has repeated this promise time and time again. During the 2011 Annual Council of Love Gathering, Universal Mother Mary repeated "I give you my essence of Blue Diamond yet again, so you will know that I am within you, around you, next to you, above, below and in every cranny and crevice in between. We are not separate. The gift of the Nova grid of humanity is unity; unity, community, and connectedness. It is the joy of knowing you are unique in any universe and you are exactly the same. It's the beauty of creation. I invite you, my sacred souls, children of my heart, to join with me to go through this portal of Oneness and beyond. It is time for your next step."

Gift of the Pink Diamond

In 2009, seven years after the deep anchoring of the Blue Diamond of healing, nurturing and beginning to work on the foundation of Nova Earth our beloved Divine Mother gifted us with the Pink Diamond energy. This energy is the activation and anchoring of our wholeness – of all aspects, a renewed grid, our soul design, and most importantly a deep unconditional connection, acceptance, acknowledgement and love of who we are, here on Earth, in form. If you cannot love yourself fully or completely, you cannot be genuinely part of community. You cannot fully experience love for others and the collective if you are not in a place of love for your sacred self.

Mother Mary explains it this way: "The gift of the Pink Diamond is to ignite that perfection of divinity. It is a state of being. And if you wish a tangible, yes then think of a Pink Diamond within your heart. It is a good place to put it and to think of it, and we will be working a lot with it during our time together. But make no error in your thinking – it is a state of being in the full divinity and the expression of that divinity, the beauty, grace, truth, and Love of who you are. Not who I am, but who you are. You are the teachers, you are the creators, you are the pathfinders, the healers, the channels. This is not a gift that I am bestowing freely upon the planet. It is not like my Blue Diamond that I have instilled upon the populous, the collective, so that they would begin to heal and know that they are loved. This is a gift to you. It is the gift from the Father and I directly to your heart."

Gift of the Golden Flame of Yahweh

This attunement first given in 2010 is the gift of the essence of the Divine Masculine, the union with the Father, with the ability to co-create and anchor in physicality upon Earth. Like the gift of the Blue Diamond from the Mother, this is the very essence of the Father.

Yahweh speaks to our hearts when He says, "I give you my Golden Flame, the flame of infinite creation, my essence which balances with the Mother's essence, and with yours. I give you my essence to balance the male and female, the divine masculine and feminine. I give it to you so you may jump forward not only in time but in joy, glee, courage, faith, and action.

"There is a lot of talk upon your planet these days about Ascension. The Ascension is simply a higher realm of consciousness, a higher realm of being – so as I instill this Golden Flame within you, I ignite that higher knowing. I give this to you from my heart to yours because you are loved and cherished, and I am your Father."

It was only with this gift and activation of the Golden Flame that I realized that there was a shadow part of myself that had skirted the fullness of this relationship with the Father. There was a part of me that knew that the Father always attended to my needs, making sure there was a roof over my head and food on the table. But I had kept it distant; more maintenance than closeness – and that was even after uniting in the heart of Father/ Mother/One. I always called upon that Energy for protection, wisdom, and 3D help but there was this unacknowledged part of me that shied back and at times felt that the Father was the old thundering God of the Old Testament. The feeling was "behave and don't get too close; don't mis-step or you will be punished." My God, what I was missing? What I had denied myself all these years?

The Golden Flame of Yahweh is where we can warm our hearts and souls. It is where we can turn to be strengthened not only with courage and stamina but with wisdom, prudence and a true knowing of the bigger picture. It is where we can go to re-ceive the infinite Love of the Father who only wishes us to shine and be happy. It is where I go when exhausted and disheartened to gather the courage to go on.

Activation of the Tri-Flame

The activation of the Golden Flame in 2010 set the stage for the completion of the activation and attunement of our Tri-Flame. The instillation of the Golden Flame completes the triad with the Blue Diamond of the Mother's essence and the Pink Diamond, the essence of "your sweet wholeness." Yahweh en-courages us, "do not forget my sweet ones to work with that Tri-Flame within your heart; the blue of the Mother, the pink of your divine self, and my gold. Balance this and let it burn brightly for it is what holds you in that place of clarity."

If there is one key to Ascension and a theme that has persist-ed since the initial opening of the 12:12 portal, it is balance. The Tri-Flame not only represents balance, it is the balancing of all of our being. It is essential preparedness for entry into the higher realms and dimensions. It is us, in all our brilliant glory, saying we have embraced all aspects of our being, all gifts, and we are ready – to fly, to ascend, to serve.

Ascension Activation & Energy Attunement

The culmination of all these gifts and preparation has come this past year, so that we may fly through the Ascension portals, claim our personal Shift into the higher dimensions and fully engage with our role, purpose and mission within the greater plan of the Mother/Father/One.

There has been and is a great deal of global discussion about the end of the Mayan calendar and the meaning of that cessation. Scholars deeply involved in the study of the Mayan calendar tell us the end of the Mayan calendar is not December 21, 2012 as so popularly thought, but rather October 28, 2011. It was the Council of Love gave the first Ascension attunements into the fifth through seventh dimensions. Forty-four of us gathered in Sedona, Ariz., in sacred ceremony and flew through that gateway. No longer bound by the illusions and false paradigms of the third dimension of lack and limitation we have anchored within the fifth to seventh dimensions and are enjoying the wonders of that reality while also fulfilling our role as way-showers and gate-keepers for those still anchored in the third.

When I began to channel the Council of Love, my life changed in many ways. One of those changes is what I call the three a.m. wake-up call. Whenever the COL wants to begin a major teaching, download or transmission they wake me up in the wee small hours of the morning, when everything is quiet, my mind is quiet and out of the way, when their voices can be heard so clearly it is as if they are standing right next to me – and of course they are. I have long learned that there is absolutely no point in trying to ignore these wake-up calls; there will be no sleep until the transmission is complete. It is a regular occurrence in our home for my husband to get up in the morning to find me crying, beaming and sleepy in front of my computer, our beloved ET angel cat, Nike, curled up next to me holding the energy. This is especially true in the months prior to our annual gathering. The tears are from the sweet loving energy and insights that flow through me, from the feeling of complete overwhelm of such knowing, and wondering "how could I have missed that?"

Therefore, it came only as a little surprise that after I had completed this book and was seeking the "perfect title" that the three o'clock wake-up call came. My working title for the book was "Ascension Now" but I kept hearing whispers it was more than that. Usually when I channel the Council of Love, I hear one voice, often many will come in but one at a time. I can count on one hand the number of times that they have come in as a whole. I believe that process is mostly in consideration for me, so as to not blow my circuits. That night was one of those exceptions.

A voice was booming in my head, and I would have sworn it was bouncing off the walls. Presences and apparitions are a common occurrence in our home, but that is a whole other story. Eyes now wide open, I inquired who as to who was speaking. A booming voice came back "The Council of Love." OK, that's enough to get me up. But they suggested "no, just lie there and listen." Honestly, at three a.m. I was happy to oblige, as they began their message to me.

"Linda, you are an awakener, you have always been an awakener. You have been awakening people for over twenty years – that is your job, your service. Understand that people awaken in many different ways. Some wake up bright, shiny and raring to go; others wake up slowly, needing to ease into the day; others wake up grumpy no matter how good a night's sleep they have had; others won't wake up until the house falls down around them; while others have insomnia and are panicked at the thought of another day. It doesn't matter – each being is unique and their way is to be honored. Your job is not to judge, just to awaken. Regardless of their reactions there is an immediate need for awakening. Do not take their reactions as personal, those belong to them not you.

"Now is the time of the Great Awakening, it is time for all to awaken and prepare for the new day, the new times upon Gaia. That is now your job, and it intensifies like never before. This wake-up call is loud and urgent. It is to be heard in every nook and cranny of your planet. There can be no avoidance, no crawling back under the covers. It is time, and this book is our instrument to awaken all who will listen."

So it is humbly and with gratitude I offer this spiritual primer to awaken you. I have written this book in a way that is straightforward and readable. It doesn't matter if you have been at your spiritual journey for years or this is the first time you have ever considered things in this way. The book's energy will take you where you need to go.

This combination of activations, attunements, gifts prepare you for a smoother ride into what we think of as the higher realms and dimensions. So please take advantage of this opportunity, open and anchor in your heart and allow the Council of Love to guide you through this Ascension process – this Shift in consciousness and being.

Your dream may have been sweet or a terrible nightmare, it matters not. Now is the time for your journey into the exciting new adventure to begin.

Chapter 1

What is Ascension?

Ascension is a gift from the heart of God. It is the opportunity to shift from the current third dimensional reality of polarity and duality to the fifth through the seventh dimensions of creation, peace and Love. It is our chance to be, to live and fulfill our soul mission and purpose, and to complete this phase of our role in the unfoldment of the Divine Plan. It is the gift of life being lived in alignment with the truth of who you are and your place within the Universe. It is not death, it is not Armageddon, and it is not "the end." It is not exclusive, a gift for only the "chosen ones" – it is a gift offered equally to every living being on this planet. It is the shedding of the old skin of Gaia and the re-birth of all of us into a higher heart-based conscious reality. Earth, Gaia, has been on this trajectory of Ascension for a long time now. The majority has not paid attention to the small shifts or drift in the polar axis but we have certainly noticed climate changes, global warming, and societal shifts

Ascension is the fulfillment of the Divine Mother's plan – the restoration of Love on Earth. The restoration of peace and harmony, where all beings have the opportunity to experience Love, joy, peace in physicality and form. It is not about abandoning human form. It is about surrendering the pattern of living from our heads instead of our hearts. In this Shift humanity is changing to a reality that is centered and guided from the heart. We are being taught to live, see and lead with our heart knowing. In many ways it is the closing of a circle begun so long ago when people did listen to their hearts, intuition, spirits and Source.

The Ascension or Shift of the planet Earth and all upon it has been planned and talked about for thousands of years. Today however, you can't look or talk to anyone who is on their spiritual path without hearing about or discussing Ascension. So the question is not only what is it, but why now? What does this Shift process look, feel, smell, and taste like? What will we experience? And most importantly, how do we do this; how do we ascend in the smoothest most graceful manner possible?

It doesn't matter if you call it The Shift, Ascension, Descension; 12:12, the end of the Mayan calendar, Divine Union, entering the fifth or seventh dimension. It's all the same. For the purposes of this book, the term Shift and Ascension are used interchangeably.

You have already been experiencing the energetic Shifts of Gaia and humanity. You have witnessed the earthquakes, tsunamis, floods, and droughts; you have witnessed the crumbling of the financial institutions, Wall Street, the housing and mortgage market, bankrupt nations – Greece, Portugal, Spain, Turkey; you have witnessed the devastation caused by the conjoining of nature and man – the Gulf of Mexico oil spill, the nuclear meltdown, and the extinction of species. You have seen the human cry for freedom as the shackles of tyranny are broken throughout the Middle East, and the attempts of political fanatics to reassert power. So how do we navigate these changes in a way that is thoughtful, considerate and kind both to ourselves, our planet and each other? What are the steps we can take to ensure not only we, but those we love and cherish, make this transition safely and soundly? Is there a guide book?

Yes there is and this is it.

The Great Awakening is the Council of Love's guidebook that will lead you through the process of understanding that will raise your vibration into the fifth and/or seventh dimension. This journey is accomplished with your active full participation through channeled information, guided mediations and energy attunements that will make this jump into the higher dimensions smooth, joyous and peaceful. This is not a book about just deadlines and dates; it is a spiritual primer to Ascension, not an appointment book.

Are you ready?

Let us begin this journey together with Lord Maitreya, our future Buddha of Love's Invitation to Ascension.

"Greetings, I am Maitreya. Welcome, welcome my brothers and sisters. I bring you greetings this day. I am Horseman of the East, Bringer of the Now, Holder of the Love and Holder of the Flame.

"There is much talk, my friends, about what is going on upon your beautiful planet and my beautiful planet as well. There is much activity within your places of power, which interests me very little, and with your star brothers and sisters, with the elementals and the kingdoms, with the waters and the oceans and the plates of Gaia. There is very little upon your planet that is not in movement right now, including yourself.

"I come this day to talk to you about the Shift. And there are many terms for this, for many of you think in terms of 12:12, many of you think in terms of Ascension. It does not matter what you call this. It is a change and a Shift to higher consciousness and Love, and it is wide open.

"This is not a selective invitation. This invitation is extended to all beings everywhere. Now I want you to think about this with me for a moment. As you read open your third eye, as I wish you to see the vision I am implanting right there in this moment. Your vision of the Shift is limited. That is all right; in fact for most of you the lesson has been to trust, to come to know that you do not need to know everything, you just need to follow your hearts, to stand back when necessary and to take action when necessary, in that beautiful harmony of your heart and your mind. Our trust in and with you is infinite.

"You live and you have always existed in an ever-expanding Universe. That does not change. That is Universal Law and we do not know of any plan, in any realm, to change that rule of expansion. It is infinite. Why do I preface my words to you in this way? I have spoken to you over the years a great deal about Universal Law and the Law of so within so without, as above so below. So I repeat, you live in an ever-expanding Universe. And therefore, my sweet ones, my angels and ET's, my elementals and fairies, you are expanding. You are expanding far greater than you know. Of course you have noticed it and I am pleased to see that many of you, most of you, are taking great joy in this, and are actively seeking to understand the nature of this expansion.

"My invitation to you this day, my guidance and my plea, is to explore your inner Universe more deeply. Because it is also a road map and a mirror for what is happening and occurring and unfolding externally upon your planet. The dark is coming to light; the light is infusing greater definition. Behaviors, situations, institutions, paradigms, are crumbling left and right, and there is no better news than that. But it also means that they are crumbling within you as well. What happens, as that occurs, is there is more space, more roominess, greater clarity, more love, and more time, or what you think of as time. Hence you are free to commit more energy to what you wish to do because you are not spending energy in worrying, fussing, thinking about what might be, what if. As you let that go into that spaciousness, the emptiness, time and energy open up for you.

"There are vast oceans within you, there are caves and mountains, yes spiritual, emotional, and they are to be explored. And you say to me 'Lord, why at a time when there is so much going on upon the planet, when everyone is bursting at the seams waiting for the unfoldment, do you guide me to go quiet, to go to the stillpoint, and go within?' Because my beloved ones, it is from the stillness and from the place of Love that you are creating externally the quiet and the Love for the unfoldment. If you are not holding it within you, who is? And if you are not holding it within you, then how does it reflect in the outer world? It is not possible. Yes, we hold that space in our realms and dimensions, your star brothers and sisters hold it as well, but your full participation is necessary.

"I ask you to use the Universal Law of Transmutation, of Transubstantiation, of Magnification and to magnify out into the world your love, your joy, your deep peace and surrender, and your knowing of the inevitable unfoldment of the Mother's plan. To be fearless, to be the servants of Archangel Michael that so many of you are, to be the colleague of St. Germaine's healing that so many of you are, to be the pink rose. None of you are single faceted. That is why so often you have been given the energies of the diamond, that you would come to see the brilliance of your multi-faceted self.

"The Shift is upon you. Often we have said 'You are ahead of schedule.' Now in any language we know what that means. You are on that wave, and as you meet the shore, you caress it with that gentleness of power.

"There is only the energy of Love and creation within the entire Universe. That is what you will find when you explore and it is what you will find at stillpoint. Everything else is illusion and that is also why I encourage you to go within. Do not get caught up in the breakdown of the illusions that are going on upon your planet. Do not get caught in the drama. Send your Love, take action where you are guided, and then stand back. Be the observer. I am the Buddha of the future, I have told you this, and I am also the Buddha of right now. I bring the messages, the energy, and the promise of unconditional Love.

"I already walk among you often. Yes, I take various forms but soon many will know me. The channel has said to look to the person standing next to you. My friends, during this Shift I look to you, for you are part of my sacred circle and I am part of yours.

"Do not fall into the fear mongering, of cataclysm, of darkness, of loss. Yes there will be a period of darkness. Stay calm. Stay within your heart. Yes there will be a loss of many lives for there are those who have simply already made the choice; they wish to depart. Why would you deny that of them when they are tired and they simply want to go home? That is the rule of compassion, to understand and not assume the burden.

"I have begun by talking about all realms. Not a great deal of attention is given to the fact that all realms are shifting in this consciousness and to this place of Love. Many of the kingdoms have already rooted and integrated the Ascension energy within; the rocks, the trees, the mountains, the birds, yes many of the beings who are four-legged. We also speak of the elementals; even your star brothers and sisters receive benefit. They come to witness and to be part of this rebirth. Of course they come in peace. They come because they have witnessed such terrible devastation, and have learned the walk of peace. But they also come to receive and to share the bounty at this table. None are denied. Some may choose not to partake, that is very different. None are denied. All are equally welcome, yes, right to the very last moment. So do not stand in judgment. Do not stand, ever, and think 'well, they're in, they're out.' That is not of Love. That is representative of the worst paradigms, which are being destroyed upon your planet. It is of control and limitation.

"Love everybody, everybody and everything you meet, you witness. No, you do not have to love their drama and actions. But honor the role they play in this unfoldment just as you wish to be honored for your role. This activation comes now. The vibration continues to be raised, it will not be halted, and it will take another quantum jump. You are preparing and will be ready.

"I am with you. I am with you in all ways and I am with you in that inner universe. Take time to explore with me; take time to know how deeply you are loved and how I love and I support you. I will sit with you for a moment or a million years, for it is the same. Go in peace my friends. Go within. Farewell."

Lord Maitreya is very clear the invitation to humanity and far beyond is wide open. It is not exclusionary; it is not just for Christians, Muslims, Jews, atheists, or Lightholders. All are welcome – the doorway is open, and the entry ticket is trust and Love. How we prepare for this entry into a new realm is by going deep within, by going into our hearts and rediscovering the Love and wisdom that lies there, by developing our trust muscles to know that we can do this – individually and collectively. This is not a difficult or daunting task. This is not about becoming a monk in a cave meditating all day. This is about becoming aware and connected in ways that perhaps you never have been. It's about taking time, a little time each day, to connect with God, Source, the Universe, the angels, the Archangels – whatever it is that speaks to your heart and from that place of quiet heart connection to listen to the messages and whispers of your heart. It's about re-discovering your joy, about waking up in the morning with a smile in your tummy and knowing you're on track and everything is right in the world.

There are people all around us, people we meet every day who live rich lives of caring and Love. They may or may not be "spiritual," they may not wear their beliefs on their coat sleeves – that doesn't mean that they are not worthy or ready to ascend. Both Jesus and Archangel Michael tell us that there will be many who run for the doorway at the last minute. It is our job to hold that door open for them. It is our job to prepare ourselves so we may be the gatekeepers and showers of the way when the time comes, and I believe the time is not long. In fact, the Ascension process has already started.

Thousands are going through the portal daily and then reaching back into the third dimension to shepherd others. It is never our role to judge who wants to come, who gets to come. Jesus Sananda tells us the only requirement is a loving heart, an open heart. Now that doesn't mean those who choose to catch the train at the last minute are going to have a smooth ride – there may well be bumps and hiccups, but don't forget not only will we be there to help, so will the Company of Heaven. But in order to do that – to fulfill our promise, we need to begin right now.

Jesus Sananda on 2012

"I am Jesus Sananda, brother of your heart and brother of your soul, brother of your journey, and I welcome all of you upon this beloved planet. I welcome you to this time of unity, connectedness and balance; I welcome you home. I welcome you home not only to the fifth dimension but the seventh, if you choose. I welcome you home to my heart. I wish to tell you and to speak to your hearts about 2012, and the upcoming years.

"I can hear you saying to me 'Lord, please whatever you do don't tell us that this chaos and turmoil will continue.' Shall I remain silent? Shall I not tell you the truth? That is not possible for me. So let me speak to you my beloved friends, this is it; this is the time when our beloved sweet Gaia ascends on her journey homeward. She spirals up into the Heart of One and down into the fifth dimension.

"It is miraculous and it is also the fulfillment of the promise made between us, particularly the Mother, the Divine Feminine, when Gaia volunteered to do this. It is her sacred journey and for millions and millions of years she has nurtured you, she has held you, she has taken care of you, even when there were times when she shrugged or adjusted. There are many who assist Gaia in this preparation and journey – your sweet selves, and yes us, your star brothers and sisters, and planetary assistance. Planetary assistance is something few of you have ever considered but there are other sentient planets that are also assisting Gaia in this undertaking.

"Gaia wants you to be with her in this sacred journey, in this journey of Oneness, of Love. And when I say 'you' I mean all of you, the trees, the water, the mountains, the air, the oceans, the birds, the snakes, the spiders, and each of you my beloved friends. She invites you to come along. And each of you, before you came to this planet, and during this reincarnation, has said 'yes, I wish to do this. I have waited so darn long for the return of Love, for the fulfillment of the plan on Earth. I am going. Nothing will stop me.'

"You have turned to me and you have pledged and you have said to me 'Jeshua, this time we will complete the journey of Love; we will anchor this journey within our hearts. And when the time is right and the activation occurs, we will be ready.' And you are, you are more than ready my beloved ones. And although you do not see me in full form yet, (although some of you do), I am with you as are the Archangels, my blessed Mother, Yahweh, the Ascended Masters, the Company of Heaven, and the Legions of Light. We are in this together. So you say to me 'Jeshua, Jesus, Sananda, what does this unfoldment look like?'

"I speak to you in global terms and while I do so, I also embed within your heart what your individual journey looks like. There will continue to be what looks like elimination or dislocation of some of the institutions, practices, environments, and ways of doing business that are not of Love. This has not changed. There is a place for commerce, for the exchange of what you create and trade; that is not a problem. There is a place for those who wish to engage in politics, but it is politics that are based on the thirteen Blessings and Virtues. It is societies that are based fundamentally on Love, that do not include the paradigms of old Earth, of greed, of lust....ah we do not even want to talk about it. So that will be fading away but at the same time many new things will be coming on.

"The new is already emerging; you see it all around you. Sometimes you turn your head and pretend not to see or are afraid to look, afraid to hope just in case it isn't real because you do not want to be duped or disappointed again. Turn and face it because this is your time and your creation with Gaia, with us. The Light grows, the energy that you hold, your crystalline body, all of this is coming on line. It is already well underway. New institutions, new understandings of what this means will also emerge, and that is important. You do not arrive in the fifth dimension as if you are going to a resort, a Club Med, or Club Galilee; it is not a five-star inclusive resort. But it will feel that way because the ability to create, to manifest, to build what you wish. To build is simple because the illusions and the density of the third dimension are gone. It is already over. Some cling to it but that does not matter because they are clinging to an illusion that is disintegrating even as they do so.

"So the mantra for this and coming years is to let it go and to embrace the wholeness of your being, to embrace the wholeness of your community, and dear hearts, your community is the human collective and everything else that is upon this Earth. It is not simply where you live; the star technology has taken care of that.

"It is necessary during this time of transition that you also make peace with the third dimension. And you say 'well what do you mean, how do I do that?' You do this by blessing everything you have known in that reality, not merely the physicality or the experience, but everything. What you have thought of as the third dimension, as duality, polarity, all of that disappears; it is gone. It simply will not exist. If you really wish to continue in that struggle then we will take you elsewhere; you will not be harmed or die, but you will be taken elsewhere.

"Our plan, our request, my Mother's plan is to invite you all; each and every one of you on this journey, on this adventure because dear hearts it is exciting. It is playful, it is fun, it is not drudgery, and it isn't something you are working at. Remember when we have sat together and laughed, played and broken bread, and created bread; that is what this journey is about, so we invite you. Do not attach and do not judge, for we all know the trouble that can cause. Do not judge what you see dissolving, disintegrating, and, whatever you do not judge your fellow human beings, for each and every one of them are bright angels on a mission. This is a time of co-creation as never before. We have done a great deal of co-creation, as have your star brothers and sisters, but it has always been in the reality that you were occupying.

"The rules change as you shift dimensions. One of the wondrous qualities of the fifth dimension is the ability to manage change, to bring forth change and your future societies; your planet is so ready. You have seen the forerunners of this. Yes, there is resistance in some sectors, but do not judge them. The key to this is to send them Love, send them Michael's Blue Flame of Truth, send them my Sacred Heart. Send them the magenta, send them the Blue Diamond of the Mother, but send to them and bless them and help them to understand the world has changed, and it has changed for the better.

"I wish you to know how much I Love you. You have not only persevered, you have not only hung on, but you have had faith and hope and you have lived this even in what you felt were the darkest nights. I honor and respect you. Please, come walk with me. Farewell."

So what's the difference between the fifth and seventh dimension – and by the way, what happened to the fourth ?

One of the challenges we face when thinking about Ascension and the Shift of dimensions is not applying the understandings or rules of the third dimension elsewhere. Our immediate reaction to considering dimensions is to think in terms of time and space continuum. That's helpful but not the full story. Albert Einstein came to me in channeling several years ago and said his work on Earth was incomplete and there were several things he would like to channel through me. Can you imagine my surprise? You might have guessed that in this life I am not a science person. I'm the one that struggled through the high school courses and then went straight for the liberal arts in college. Nevertheless, here's Einstein, hair flying, eyes twinkling saying he wants to be part of the team and talk about healing and dimensions. What can a girl do but say "yes?"

Albert Einstein has given us a description of how to think about the dimensions. Although current scientists have come up with eleven dimensions their information is incomplete. There are twelve dimensions available within the human experience and within each of those dimensions there are twelve planes or levels. What I would like to do here is have Einstein describe the dimensions and then come back to the question about the differences between the fifth and seventh dimensions, and where we are headed in the Ascension process, including what do we feel and experience, what does it look like to we wee humans.

Albert Einstein – The Nature of Life and Dimensions on Earth

"Humans usually think of dimensions in terms of measurement. The term "measurement" refers to length, width, depth in the third dimension, with the added element of time is the fourth, and numeric assignment to the fifth. I wish you my dear friends to think of dimensions in a different way – not excluding measurement but as a measurement of growth and qualities of being; states of existence. As humans you have come to consider growth as the core definition of what is alive – what is living. Examples of this would be trees, plants, animals, crystals, and of course human beings. It is natural for you to think of yourselves as the top rung of the food chain of life which expresses in the third dimension.

"What you and I failed to realize is that life, life forms, and dimensions are not a ladder but rather a circle. That circle of twelve dimensions, each with twelve planes, defines this Universe in which all life forms participate, or have the capacity to participate.

"Each dimension has qualities, or growth patterns, that define it. That is the concept of dimensional measurement; you are measuring the energy force of that quality. Each of these dimensions has their own signature as it were, and, of course, within this there is a gradation – much the same way a diamond has a gradation. I wish to discuss these but first I outline them. But before I do it is necessary to put your preconceptions and judgments about ascendancy aside. Each dimension has a plethora of gifts or learning opportunities – opportunities for evolution on the physical and spiritual scale. What you also have need to realize is that all of these dimensions operate and are observable in the third dimension. One of the qualities of the third dimension is the ability to observe all dimensions and realities in the physical life form. Now it is time to pay attention to what is being represented to you but that you have not adequately observed. I suggest this to you because that is part of the process of being born into the third dimension – it is the possibility and the responsibility to observe like a scientist.

First Dimension

"The first dimension is amorphous, having no defined or classified form. Believe it or not ideas fall into this categorization. Ideas are simply a chemical electro-magnetic event. Ideas have no physical substance until such time as they are brought into action and form. You have an experience of this dimension when you are brain-storming or free-associating, letting ideas move and circulate throughout the inter-dimensional field. That is why so often there are similar concepts or scientific discoveries at the same time. It is from this place that the understanding of the one hundredth monkey, of how ideas are seemingly simultaneously transmitted to the collective emerges. Both the first and second dimensions hold the qualities of humility and prudence.

Second Dimension

"The second dimension has the aspect of flat spatial extent, meaning that there is no depth and therefore often not perceived by the human eye. The quality of this dimension is the ability to mutate, grow and evolve from one amorphous mass into another and so on. These are often micro-organisms, virus or bacteria, such as a common cold. Cancer also falls into this dimension – evolving from a cell and often mutating into a tumor or growth. Usually the life form of the second dimension is only observable under a microscope – but the presence of this life form is clearly evidenced both in nature and within your physical bodies. This dimension teaches inter-dependence as life forms are dependent upon a host whether it is a human form, air, water and so on.

"There are many life forms that inhabit this Universe who are of this nature, popping in and out depending on whether they are facing you or not. Not many of them inhabit your planet, but one example is of the Serros (alien parasites) who feed energetically upon humans. This is not a malign activity but simply an interdependence that one life form must attach to another in order to survive. The quality of this life form, similar to the first, is that there is no experience of emotion. It is learning to simply be in form and learn interdependence without the presence of emotion.

"What many of the scientists are defining in String Theory as the other eleven dimensions are in fact aspects of the twelve planes of the second dimension. They have not yet made the quantum leap to understanding that dimensions are not defined by physicality but by qualities of growth.

Third Dimension

"The third dimension as you are aware is defined by the quality of the perception or experience of physicality – meaning the universe is perceived through the experience of length, width, depth. But the growth quality is the ability to embrace all dimensions, realities, emotion and spirit. It also has the unique quality of freedom of choice. All of the numerically higher dimensions have the opportunity to exhibit in the third. The growth opportunity and quality of the third is the ability to choose to expand beyond the mere perception of physicality, and, incorporate all aspects of self.

"This is what the Universal Mother talks about when She is discussing incorporating all aspects of self. The third dimension is not limited by the time-space continuum, it merely appears to be. That is the challenge and the opportunity in the third to reach beyond physical appearances.

Fourth Dimension

"The fourth dimension is the quality of magic, what many of you think of as alchemy. It is the growth into the realization and action of being an agent for transformation, transmutation and transubstantiation. This dimension is very easily accessible from your third and is witnessed continually by living divas, fairies, elementals and so on. It is important for you to realize that once you have anchored this growth component within yourself, i.e., once you have anchored the fourth dimension lessons and growth within your being, these beings and abilities will be not only visible but commonplace. An everyday human example of this dimension, and one which bothered me throughout my human life was the splitting of the atom. What you think of as science is often simply operating within this dimension.

Fifth Dimension

"The fifth dimension is the ability to cope, create, manage

and manipulate change. This channel, Linda Dillon, has often spoken of the fifth dimension where the quality of change is constant. That is correct but the rationale behind this is that the being is learning how to deal with and create change. It is the precursor to creation. You live in an infinite Universe, one that is constantly in the process of change and growth. If you are not able to manage change internally and externally then you cannot incorporate the qualities of the higher dimensions with grace. Therefore the growth aspect of the fifth is the ability to move through change, manipulating it in ways that are loving, kind, considerate of self and the collective, and respectful of the grander plan of unfoldment.

"There has been a great deal of discussion about the Earth, Terra Gaia, moving into the fifth dimension. This speaks to a fundamental misunderstanding of the quality of dimensions. The dimensions are not fixed points on a compass. They are a circle dancing, moving and expanding constantly. There is constant movement with and between all dimensions – they are fluid. The plant, animal and human kingdoms collectively have been intensely learning the lessons of constant change. What do you think the explosion in technology, human advances and thinking has been about? The human community has managed enormous change in the past few hundred years. No, not always well or wisely; but that is the nature of the dimension – it offers the opportunity to learn the growth lessons of that dimension. Gaia who operates at a very different frequency and time/space continuum from humans has conquered the lessons of change eons ago. So have most of the other kingdoms.

"So when there is discussion about moving from one dimension to another, simply think of it as moving from one classroom to another, passing from one grade to another, while understanding that sometimes you have to go back and review basic principles in order to remind yourself what you learned and forgot. You do not eliminate the spatial and time continuum because you are moving inter-dimensionally. You are expanding yourself while remaining in the form and expression of the third dimension.

"The qualities of growth that occur as part of the Shift in and through the fifth dimension are patience, stamina, humor, and wisdom that the more things change the more they are constant. Love and joy are constants my friend. And by the way, why would you think these blessings and qualities are the exclusive purview of the third dimension. That is truly human ego.

Sixth Dimension

"The sixth dimension is the one that is my favorite – it is the place or state of being where ideas and belief systems mutate into form. This dimension has often been defined by this channel as the dimension of chaos. There are many above and below who would suggest that the human race collectively is in the process of experiencing the growth opportunities of the sixth. When we say chaos we speak of it in terms of creative chaos – for in every chaotic situation – whether it is internal such as cancer or external such as war or societal breakdown, there is an opportunity for growth. Often you have heard me speak of the process of implosion/explosion of creation. Chaos is the nucleus for that action and outcome. It can be beautiful and magnificent – think of it as the Big Bang, think of it as the birth of a solar system, the death of a star.

"The biggest opportunity for growth of the sixth dimension is the understanding that you are not in control. It brings with it the growth of the qualities of surrender, trust, fortitude and hope. It is the ability to acknowledge that seemingly random chaos has a Divine patterning. It teaches the lessons of reaping what you sow. it brings forth a profound appreciation of the gift of the unknown.

Seventh Dimension

"The seventh dimension is known as the dimension of the Christ consciousness. This is the state of being in the heart and knowing of Love. It is the growth opportunity for compassion, kindness, selflessness, honoring and Love. When you anchor in this place of consciousness you are fully capable of holding the vibrations, energies, lessons, understandings and growth of all of the twelve dimensions available to you on this planet. It is the gentle allowing state of being that permits expansion and incorporation of your entire original imprint, soul design – what you think of as your universal or higher self, your angelic self or your higher self.

"If you think of the seventh dimension in terms of the electro-magnetic field that governs your planet, it allows you the capacity to incorporate the electric nature of the energy, patterning and lessons of the first six dimensions, and, the magnetic energy pull of the eighth through twelfth dimensions. You can think of the seventh dimension as the place of still point where all energies anchor and flourish. It can be the place of intersection of all, and is the most natural and comfortable dimension for human beings because it is not only peaceful but feels like home to most. It is the state of being in perfect balance, of simply being. While many dimensions entail action, this is more a state of allowing. Because it is the place of intersection, it is the growth lesson of acceptance and acknowledgement of unity and connectedness of all beings, all dimensions, and all life forms.

Eighth Dimension

"The eighth dimension quality is creation. This is the state of being where the manipulation of energy, of my beloved sub-atomic particles, of the fuel of Love into form – be it process or tangible, is learned. When you have anchored the growth pattern of the eighth, then you have no difficulty in bringing forth consistently that which your heart desires and that which is alignment with Source and your Universe. Creations that are not in alignment with the higher self and collective are phantoms manufactured by human ego and not of the sacred nature of the growth patterns of the eighth.

"In many ways, this is the most challenging growth cycle of all. Many travel through this creation dimension again and again shying away from the energy because it entails use of personal core essence power, and the acceptance of responsibility. This lesson of acceptance for one's creations is an inherent component of this growth cycle. You cannot consistently create and anchor into the third reality without acceptance of this precept. Many shy away from this cycle because they believe it is a sin of hubris to think that they can manipulate atoms. They believe that this is the purview only of the gods. This situation is often present because of flow from past lives, when human ego manufactured painful experiences.

"The qualities of this growth are the understanding of unity with One and All, the ability to fully embrace and participate with God Source. It is an acceptance of your role within the Universe, and it is a humble devout vow to abide by the Universal Laws of creation. It is through the embracing of this growth cycle that the anchoring of Nova Being and the creation of Nova Earth will truly come to pass. The virtue is awe, in deep recognition of the wonder and unlimited potential of the Universe and Source.

Ninth Dimension

"The ninth dimension growth pattern engenders completion. This is often a challenge for human beings. It is the understanding of the pattern of growth for each cycle of life and existence. It is the embracing of completion while realizing that while life cycles are defined, existence is infinite. It is anchored and made manifest in the human being by the ability to let go, to reach resolution, to continue on in joy, to accept and participate in the unfoldment. The quality of this dimension is truth.

"The growth pattern of this dimension is easily discernible in human beings. The most significant anchoring of this dimension's quality is when a baby is born. They choose, consciously and fully aware, to relinquish their state of angelic freedom to come into form, to continue with a new cycle in order to be of service and have a unique human experience. That momentous event could not take place unless the spirit coming into form had fully embraced the qualities of the ninth. That is what humans so often fail to understand – that the growth patterns of the other dimensions are already present within the third dimension when the child is born. They are as undeniable as the rings on an ancient oak tree – not seen from the outside but present nevertheless. It is the truth of the core essence. The choice in the human third reality is simply whether or not you will allow those qualities to be brought to the surface. The same quality is seen in the completion of life – of the ability to resolve and embrace the next chapter of existence. The same is true of the growth patterns of resolution of old patterns, relationships, habits, addictions, and jobs. When you practice completion you are drawing on the energy of the ninth dimension. You are pulling to you the knowledge and patterning of that reality.

Tenth Dimension

"The tenth dimension contains the growth patterns of beauty, purity and charity. It is the patterning and state of being in complete willingness to share and participate in and throughout the Universe. It is the growth of selflessness and generosity. It is the sense and patterning of understanding, knowing and creating beauty from the purity of heart, soul, being. It is the commitment to be only a reflection of Love. This is a magnificent dimension that few upon the Earth seldom achieve but which is completely available to each of you to experience. It is so far beyond what you conceive of in terms of tangible human creation and yet is part of the pattern of each and every plant, animal, tree, rock, stream, and molecule of air on your planet. It is part of the essence of Gaia. It is the ability to fully participate uniquely but with no sense of ego-self. In many ways it embodies the quality of Divine Creation. This is the dimension where angels play.

Eleventh Dimension

"The eleventh dimension contains the growth opportunity of mastery. This term is greatly misunderstood. What mastery means is the full embrace of all abilities, knowing, and talents (of which the human are minor) of self as reflection of Divine. It is the quiet acceptance of self as participant and reflection of God Source. It is the lesson of letting go of all preconceptions and limitations and becoming a willing participating vessel of One. Now, you begin to see just how fluid the dimensions are – how they work like a formula together, joining together in growth patterns to create something new, old, unique and common. All your master teachers, including Jesus Sananda, emanate from the eleventh dimension. It is a growth pattern that when anchored results in not only the ability but the desire to teach, contribute and heal. The presence of many masters upon the Earth is a wonderful way in which to understand how the qualities of the dimensions are anchored in the third physical life-form.

Twelfth Dimension

"The twelfth dimension growth pattern is of joy, grace and Love. This is the point of wholeness where there is no need to demonstrate in form. This is the place, the state of being, and the bridge, to the Divine ecstasy. It is the place of arrival, integration and departure from your Universe. When you have integrated the growth opportunities of the twelfth dimension you are free to basically travel where you wish. It is the state of being that incorporates all the growth patterns of the other dimensions. It is outside of the time-space continuum.

"To sum up, I wish you to understand that within each of these dimensions there are twelve levels – bands or planes. This is the gradation of a diamond that I spoke of earlier. Sometimes the diamond is exceptionally clear and flawless, other times it is not. Each of these dimensions has a pattern – an observable form. Meanwhile, you are able to see this every single day not only in the unseen realms but in the humans around you. Notice how this one seems to be able to resolve, let go and complete, or that one holds quality, clarity and truth; while another seems to have learned and incorporated the growth pattern of creation.

"On this planet, and within metaphysical circles, there is a tendency to say that other inter-dimensional star beings come from a certain dimension. Understand what is being said is that group or individual carries the imprint or quality, the signature, of completing that dimension growth cycle. They are still manifesting and operating into the third dimension. Think of it as a form of multi-location.

"This understanding of the different dimension is essential to understanding your own soul design – the patterning you carry within your sacred self always. It is also crucial to building and incorporating all aspects of your being, of choosing and incorporating the qualities of each of the dimensions available to you within your Universe.

"My invitation to you is not to choose what dimension you wish to live in, but to rather embrace all the dimensions and growth patterns available to you. That is the gift to this Universe and this planet. You are a multi-dimensional being. You always have been. Now is the time to realize and embrace this miracle, this gift of you."

When you think of Einstein's descriptions it shifts the whole notion and discussion regarding Ascension. So now let's return to the fifth versus the seventh and what ever happened to the fourth question. Keep in mind what Einstein says about the dimensions and planes of each dimension being fluid – they expand and contract according to where we are as well as what is going on in this universe. What that means in practical terms is that the Shift or Ascension is not like the snap of an elastic band. Rather it is the extension of our individual and collective beings into a different sphere of experience and reality. The lessons and experience we and of course Gaia are choosing to have on our spiritual journey are changing – it is part of our collective spiritual growth and evolution. That doesn't make it any less incredible but it certainly puts it in perspective, and makes it more manageable.

Earth has been moving up the golden spiral through the fourth dimension and into the fifth for years. That Shift began slowly but surely when Earth was given her new golden grid by the Archangels back in 2002. Take a minute and listen to your heart. Look at the magic and alchemy not only in your life but in the world around you. Look at how people now see and perceive what was previously not readily open to us. We joke about it but we do perceive energies both seen and unseen differently than we did a decade ago – evidence the growth and acceptance of energy healing, of angels, of fairies, of the knowing of one's ability to consciously create with the Universe. We relate to the kingdoms, of animals, trees, plants and certainly with Gaia differently, in a more conscious participatory manner. We fully realize the inter-connectedness of all systems and that the "unexplained" really is part of everyday life.

Similarly we have become experts at managing and creating change in the past four to five years. Look at the election of Barack Obama almost fifty years after the promise of Dr. Martin Luther King Jr., the demise of the financial systems as we know them, the Arab Spring, the rise of China. If these situations are not evidence of massive change –of both creation and change management, then what is? The blockage is that we don't think of it that way. We don't stop and say – oh – this is a fifth dimensional issue making itself known. This is a fifth dimensional opportunity. Too often our response is to fall into judgment and blame of random chaos, cabals or Illuminati and not really look at what is being presented – huge opportunities for growth and creation. And that type of response drags us right back into the delusion of the third dimension of Old Earth, of polarity and duality. Who wants to stay there – certainly not Gaia. She's on her way to the seventh, that place of stillpoint and balance, the place of the Christ Consciousness and Love. Don't you want, desperately want, to go with her?

So here's the deal. Just as we all have been expanding our energy fields with the incredible waves of Love and downloads that have been penetrating the entire planet in the past few years and intensely in the last two, so has Gaia. She, and we, no longer fit neatly into that third dimensional continuum. Gaia is ascending upwards or sideways if you keep that image of the circle of dimensions, into a new spectrum of being. She is moving classrooms. She is anchoring for the moment in the fifth dimension while we anchor those blessings and virtues of change management but she is also holding the doorway open and occupying the space of the 6th and seventh dimensions. We aren't consciously aware of that Shift because we aren't there yet. But this is her plan, and it is the plan of the Divine Mother. The plan is not to arrive in the fifth dimension and just stay there – it is to keep on going until we reach what feels most like home to all of us. That offer is not time-limited, there is not a deadline about when you have to have fully shifted into each of these spaces. But you need to know physicality on Earth has shifted and will continue to shift; therefore there are actions you need to take to be part of that change if you chose to continue to live here. So the question is are you up for the ride? Of course you are!

Archangel Michael has shared a great deal of information about the human details of the Shift – what does it feel like, what do we experience, and how do we know that we've "arrived." When you consciously begin your Ascension process through prayer, meditation, ritual and attunements you will feel a sense of disassociation upon returning or opening your eyes. Dizziness, nausea, headaches are frequently experienced as well. But these symptoms of shifting usually last only a few hours, in some cases days. So it is important to heed the "do not operate heavy machinery" warning and not drive or even walk until you feel grounded.

Grounding into the heart of Gaia is essential for this Ascension process. Don't forget you are going with her – this is not an individual journey even though it can be an individual undertaking. So feel yourself dropping your red cord from the root chakra or tip of your tailbone and let in flow downward through the floor, the cement, the foundation, the Earth, the gaseous layers directly into the heart of Gaia, and keep that cord anchored as firmly as the Queen Mary. It is literally your life-line.

After the anchoring, then comes the good part – the gifts, the vision, the clairaudience, the feeling of deep connection and clarity. It feels like an expansion of gifts or abilities you have always had but perhaps were not consciously aware of having. I have had many reports of seeing, talking, visiting with the Ascended Masters, the Archangels and personal guides. There have been numerous reports of a deepened connection to Gaia, of a new awareness and clear vision of the Cities of Light.

What I am observing are two things – first the opening of awareness channels appears to be connected to the individual's mission and purpose. For example if a person is an Earth-keeper there is a deepened connection and clarity with Gaia and all of the Earthly kingdoms. If the mission is of a starseed then the connection to your star brothers and sisters, awareness and communication with them is further opened and available. Many report very clear experiences of being on board ships.

The second observation is that those who are allowing and surrendering to the experience of the Ascension process appear to be faring better – the movement is more fluid, more graceful, more joyous, filled with greater clarity and ease. Because the changes are subtle, because this isn't about the Big Bang, those who are waiting or perhaps wanting to wake up in a whole new world are experiencing disillusion and disappointment, even depression. Which of course pulls them back right down into the duality of the very third dimension.

The sensation of being in the fifth dimension or higher is one of being grounded in Gaia in the fifth but of reaching back through an open portal or trans-dimensional window into the third. You reach back to assist those on their journey forward. But there is a word of caution – do not allow yourself to be pulled back into that reality. Remember that you are in a free-will zone and that if you choose to re-enter the quagmire of the third then you are most certainly permitted. The question is why would you want to? If the answer is the human addiction to drama, the need to clear a little more, then gently do so and continue onward. The more you practice being in the fifth or higher, the easier that becomes.

Chapter 2

The Thirteenth Octave

What is The Thirteenth Octave?

The Thirteenth Octave is a state of being in Divine Union, wholly and completely anchored, and aware of being anchored, in the heart of One. It is being in alignment with the heart, mind and will of God. The gift of the Thirteenth Octave is enormous. It literally changed not only my world but the lives of thousands of people who have said "yes" and stepped forward to join in this state of Union.

In addition to the initiation and re-connection, the gifts of the Thirteenth Octave are plentiful. Each time the Thirteenth Octave sacred ceremony has taken place the Council has bestowed a gift, ability or tool to assist us in our spiritual journey here on Earth. We have been armed with an array of gifts and tools such as Universal Mother Mary's gift of removal, Mary's cloak of invisibility, Gabriel's golden infinity, Archangel Uriel's Silver Flame, Archangel Michael's sword and shield, Yahweh's keys to the warehouse of heaven. The list is enormous, in keeping with our human desire for tricks and tools, diversity and choice. But each gift is designed to assist us in completing our missions here on Earth with grace, Love, and joy.

One of the best explanations of the Thirteenth Octave comes from Archangel Gabrielle. "The Thirteenth Octave is a place, a state of being beyond what had previously been known upon your planet, in terms of conscious awareness. Previously, one would have left physical form – die, to have this experience. The referenced Thirteenth Octave is sound, for it is the point at which vibration and sound is the sound of God, beyond hearing, beyond human ears, but clearly felt throughout the Universe."

Our curious selves have always pursued the question of what will it be like, what does it feel like, afterward we will be really creative beings for having been through the Thirteenth Octave initiation? One participant put it this way, "Not much has been said about what we will really be like, what we will be able to do, what we are supposed to do, how long it's going to take for us to adjust and to actually begin utilizing the benefits, the gifts that are being given to us. I think all of us would like to know a little bit more about that if you would be so kind."

Archangel Gabrielle's reply to these questions reminds us that the first and ever-present gift of the Thirteenth Octave is the ability to heal people's hearts.

"You are given the gift of remembering how to heal the hearts of others beginning with yourself. The rate at which this occurs will be different depending on the acceptance and personality factors of each. So for some it will be instantaneous combustion, others it will be weeks, for they edge slowly into the center of the flower. When you edge back out, or when you walk back out, you have the ability to access universal information, intelligence, wisdom, knowledge, Love, truth, beauty.

"It is not that we cram your heart and soul and mind with facts, figures and experience. Rather, we give you connection for full access to all that is required, desired, needed, wished for, and available. It always has been thus, but humans, as a race, have never actively sought this union. When you finish this initiation and return to your world, you have a choice whether or not to share the gifts you have received here. To not share would render the gifts meaningless. Understand that the touching (connecting) another's heart is a practice, a meditation, that must be done consciously every day. So as you walk within your corridors of your life remember your conscious agreement, and, extend your hand and touch the hearts of those whom you encounter."

The Original Thirteenth Octave Articles

This journey into the realm of the Thirteenth Octave begins with seven of the original articles channeled by the Council of Love in order to help us understand the full significance of this portal opening. The articles were channeled sequentially over a period of about a year beginning in Fall of 1997 when the energy of the Thirteenth Octave became available. The final channeling is a current update on the Thirteenth Octave and clarification of where we collectively stand now in terms of that progression and process.

The energies of transmutation and transubstantiation have increased radically over the past year and particularly in the past several months – so how you perceive and what you receive from these channelings will be different than if you had read them initially in 1997. Additionally, the energy within every channeling in this book has been amplified to the level necessary for Ascension. So please, let the energy and information seep gently into you. I am amazed as I re-read these articles the effect of this information and how I perceive them now in a different light. Everything the Council has ever spoken about from the grid to creation to Ascension is here in those first transmissions. That fact awakens awe in me. It touches my heart and being in ways that make me understand there is really a grander plan, an unfoldment which we have chosen to be part of eons ago.

The purpose of this initial series of articles is to open your hearts and assist you in understanding the magnitude and gifts of entry into the Thirteenth Octave. The articles are bound to raise some questions – they're intended to. Write them down, make notations in the margins. Each sentence is packed so pay attention and ask the Council, ask your guides, ask your friends, but think about it, absorb the information and energy and discuss it freely and with an open heart.

The Doorway Beckons

"Greetings from the Council of Love. I am Jesus Sananda.

The doorway to the Thirteenth Octave beckons you. The opening is premature but it has been accomplished through a miracle, a gift of Love from our One Divine Being to your divine being, united in heart. It is our dearest wish that you enter, it is why you have prepared and endured all the trials, tribulation and chaos of this and many lifetimes. The answers to the universal questions that have plagued you lie beyond this gateway. This opportunity is unique in the experience of your planet, it has never occurred. You are presented with an invitation engraved with the lettering of the celestial stars, the energy of the Divine. Those of you who intend to enter know who you are, and will resonate throughout your entire being to this message.

"The Thirteenth Octave is beyond your concept of time or space; it is completely beyond your grid or the grid of physicality. It is beyond your dimension. It is the state of being united with God – All which is, All that ever could be, All that ever has been. The cycle of the twelve existences, the twelve planes that the human race is able to experience will continue for the many on Earth who do not choose or are not as yet prepared to enter this state of being. But for those who have chosen long ago, who have been encoded with the genetic and soul desire to enter, the doorway is opened to the next level, the next circle of existence.

"One of the primary reasons for the opening of the doorway at this time is because of the spiritual progress and self-sacrifice of Gaia. Through her mission of service, in harmony and in conjunction with those aligned with her energy grid, she has catapulted herself to the end of possible experience within your grid. She seeks entry to a new octave, a completely different realm of existence. Her prayers have been heard and answered, and hence the doorway has been unsealed. Those of you who wish to travel with her to the Thirteenth Octave need to do so as quickly as possible. Clear yourself of all blockages and debris, enter into the state of Love and serenity, and align with the Light. The doorway is opened, and time, in the very practical sense of which it is applied on Earth, is of the essence. Earth will exist in the seventh dimension and walk in a new reality.

"When I spoke so long ago of Love, it was never Love of

anything in particular, it was simply Love. The time has arrived for the vibration of pure Love to be permanently anchored upon this planet, and within the hearts of all who inhabit her. When you enter the Thirteenth Octave, you unite with Love, for that is all there truly is. From that place of expansion those who enter through the gateway will begin to travel back to Earth to assist those who continue the path of 12:12. It will not be the same as your earlier travels and transitions, it will not be through your emotional, physical or mental bodies for these will be transmuted, reintegrated with the whole. It will be back through the energy fields of the dimensions, back into the hearts of humans, animals, flowers, of all beings, to touch their hearts, to brush them within the gentle knowing of Love, to spark that essence within them that they may expand to the point of fully knowing the wholeness of the existence with One.

"In the distant future there will be a time when all go to the Thirteenth Octave. At that point the planet and those upon it will simply become the brilliant gold, only sheer energy; sheer light and it will be done. But it begins now with a small few who have this opportunity. However, all are told of the vision so they will travel their path and know that there is assistance, guidance and hope. It is the lack of hope, the lack of dreams that have held so many on this planet away from Love, away from the wholeness of their being, which has kept them in the illusion of separateness.

"Wholehearted surrender, not to God but to self is necessary for entry into the Thirteenth Octave. It is the most selfish act and the most selfless undertaking; it is the leap of faith, the believing in the miracles of Love with absolutely no evidence. But those who have chosen, who have nominated themselves long ago, they are fully capable of this exit and entry. They are not alone; look through the door, we all await you, yes thirteen holy ones for certain but also the entire Legion of Light. It is a welcome home party, all has been prepared. Afterward, you will go back through the door altered and whole to assist others in their journey as well. None will be left unaided, even those who refuse will be aided by the light penetrating the darkness. There will be many miracles to observe, prepare and enter.

The Apostle James continues on the subject of the magnificent opening of the Thirteenth Octave, including insights on what clearing is necessary beforehand, as well as what to anticipate physically.

"I am James the Apostle of Our Lord Jesus Christ, Savior, Son of Yahweh, greetings. I am Master of the Green Ray, guardian of the sacred doorway, portal to the heart. Much as the seventh dimension is the dimension of Love, the dimension of wholeness, the dimension where all who exist with the purpose and existence and unity of Love come to be, the Thirteenth Octave is the place for the Ascension of that Love beyond any conscious reality.

"When one moves beyond dimension, or when there is physical movement or manifestation back and forth between dimensions within the physical, then there is a pureness of being, a sheer energy field emerges. This is the existence of the Thirteenth. One cannot enter that state unless they are one with Love. This entails a total and complete clearing of past, of future, of all existence, and, unification with heart. Only then can you move through. That is why all are not entirely prepared for movement past the doorway. The ticket is clarity.

"If there is debris, the tinniest speck of doubt, one would literally decompose. The energy is this strong; stronger than anything that has previously been felt upon your planet. So while your feet will remain embedded on this Earth, your higher chakras from the heart upward will exist elsewhere. It is an extension that will leave you breathless. So, as you learn to clear know that it is essential for you to also expand. Clearing is meant to expand, not to decompress. If there was one preparation for the movement through this portal it would be to breathe, breathe the green and gold of my ray. Know that it is beginning for you now; the invitation is now in your hands.

"On the physical plane, entry through the doorway can be individual or as a group, it matters not. On this plane you must pass through one at a time, it is not a group exercise; it is a soul/sole journey. In meditation I, or an ascended one who is in harmony with you, will come and walk through the portal where we will be greeted by our only host, the Heavenly Son. The process of initiation on the other side will be slightly different for each individual, but know that it will entail an energy transfer from the circle of thirteen to the individual who stands in the center of the circle. On the outer circle there will be a spiral or coil, all the Legions of Light and the Council of Love will surround you. Following the initiation with your thirteen masters, you will enter the spiral in a clockwise motion and return by coming back into the circle to join again with me and exit.

"You will return with gifts of energy, but understand everything will have changed. There will never be a similar feeling to how you now exist. The primary gift you will bring back is a gift of the healing heart; simply by looking at another and esoterically touching their heart you will open them. You will see a transparent energy flowing clearly upon a grid. This type of vision can be used for seeing heart blockages regardless of where they are located on the grid. You will be able to see clearly who you are dealing with. There can be no hiding from someone from the Thirteenth, it is impossible.

"However, those from the Thirteenth can be invisible when they choose. These are the true rewards but you will have other gifts of magic as well because it is all one thing. Know that upon returning you will also be an anchor for the seventh dimension. The Earth has moved but all is hovering, none of the energy has been anchored. There is need for anchoring. This is a time of birthing and know there is a time when the energy could move backwards pulled by the denseness of the energy of those who sit upon her. That is why we all are buoying Gaia up at this time. Everyone is encouraged to do so. That is why there is a huge need for heart opening and surrender to Love. The more of you who pass through the more the energy will be anchored, and, the firm commitment to Ascension will anchor.

"Only those who have completely cleared will be allowed access to the Thirteenth Octave. Invitations have already been issued although not all are yet consciously aware. It is not clear, given the choice of free will, how many will join but there is immediate opportunity for many within this window of opportunity. It is interesting to us how there are beings who hold a high enough vibration that the opportunity is open to them but who choose not to move. It is a chance to be of such service to so many souls created by the same spark of Light from which we all emanate; it is strange that some will refuse. And some will not be clear enough to complete. But there will be others who will leap ahead, the ones you would term dark horses, who in Light, Love and joy will spread that vibration not only on Earth but throughout the Universe. This energy moves far beyond the planet, when we say it is off the grid understand that it is far off the planetary grid."

Archangel Gabrielle steps forward once again to share with us a deeper understanding of the nature of the Thirteenth Octave.

"Greetings, I am Gabrielle, herald of God and messenger of One. Know that the octave of which we speak is similar to all other octaves. Think of an octave as a universal system of measurement for the process of the beginning and completion of a spiritual undertaking. The process that the Earth has been involved in to date has been the process of the seventh and 8th octave; the completion of the 8th having just taken place. Know that this reference is solely for Earth, for there are those who sit upon her who participate in other octaves as well. It is similar to being in school; you can be in the eighth grade but take classes elsewhere. However, none on your planet have ever been past the ninth prior to this time; the Thirteenth has not been available to you. So it is a new undertaking for many, including Gaia.

"The doorway of which we speak began opening in June 1997 and will be fully opened in December of this year (1997). If there is not an acceptance by a significant number of hearty souls to accept this invitation to enter and anchor into the Thirteenth Octave, then it is uncertain whether this doorway will remain open. The doorway will be open for the rest of the population at a much later date, the timing of which has yet to be determined but it will be well into the 2000s.

"The purpose of this rather small group passing through the doorway to the Thirteenth Octave at this time is for those who have self-elected to enter into a state of wholeness, complete awareness by and through association not only with their thirteen Ascended Masters but with the entire Legions of Light, in order to return to Earth and assist others in their spiritual journey. It is part of their service contract, their commitment to the Divine. They have chosen long ago to travel the spiritual expressway rather than enjoy the scenic route. It is a soul decision to act as a catalyst for the unfoldment of the Divine Plan. There has been much preparation, not only in this lifetime but for eons. The miracle of the early opening has occurred. The time is now. The invitations are issued and the guests assembled, plan and intend from the deepest core of your being to attend. Go in peace."

As if this incredible invitation to enter into the Thirteenth Octave was not enough, the three a.m. wake-up calls continued. The urgency with which these messages were transmitted was, and still is, incredibly intense. The next article, A Time of Decision, almost demanded that we make a choice of how we wish to proceed, and to make that decision immediately. The hardships and the chaos is exactly what we have been experiencing in the past decade plus, but the invitation is being re-issued once again by Archangel Gabrielle. She never minces her words. The message is clear – decide whether you are in or out and get going.

A Time of Decision

"Greetings from the Council of Love. I am Gabrielle, Herald of God and Messenger of One. I come this day to speak to all Lightworkers not only across North America but across the world, of Love and joy, of a new way of being. The time for indecision must come to an end. There is no longer an envelope in time, as you know it, in which to decide whether to go ahead slowly, rapidly, or at all. One must decide now if you choose to enter the Thirteenth Octave or to remain in the cycle of 12:12. Know that this decision is one based on soul desire and purpose.

"The choice made long ago is that you would return to Earth during the time of changes, during the time of the golden age which now commences, during the time of dramatic upheaval within and throughout your planet and the Universe. The decision to be of service to the One, to be of the Love and of the Light is known clearly within your heart and the heart of the Mother. Fear not. Your intent is as clear as your photo ID to those who walk the path of righteousness, truth and wisdom.

"The issue is not who you are but how you wish to proceed. The time has come to choose not only the timing of your journey, but where you wish to remain and reside for the coming millennium. No, we do not say that there will not be relocation from time to time, but travel and relocation will be more difficult in the coming times for a variety of reasons, not simply the Earth changes which now begin in earnest.

"I have sounded my trumpet several times and many have heeded my call, each responding to the sound that vibrated within their soul. Know that my trumpeting, my tone, is the sound of God. Sometimes it calls those who have soul desire to return home. There are times when it is a call to action, and there are times when it is a call to stand as still as the rocks of ages. Now, the purpose of my trumpeting is to sound the arrival of a new way of being, a new dawn of hope and a new ray of existence, which will benefit all, not simply those who remain on Earth, and not simply those who heed the call to the Thirteenth Octave.

"We tell you that the time of duality has come to a close, and we are now in a very brief period of division – not in the sense of the wheat from the chaff, for that is not of Love and wholeness. When we speak to you of the time of division, we speak of the time when there will be decision, tacit for some, about whether to remain on Earth or whether to return home to our side. There will be further division among you who choose to remain on Earth. Do you choose to remain on the 12:12 path of spiritual existence, doing so in hardship and suffering in the days ahead or do you choose to seek a place a safety? Know, children of our heart, that the decision is not as easy as it would appear.

"Know that many of you have volunteered long ago to remain in the places of upheaval, to understand more deeply that process and to assist the Earth and those who walk upon her during the times of changes. So it is not simply a matter of "getting out of town," it is a matter of going deeply within your heart and knowing your purpose, and, aligning clearly with that purpose.

"When we say you may remain in the places of hardship and suffering, understand that this does not necessarily mean that you will come to harm, injury or death. It simply means that you have chosen to locate in a place of confusion and chaos to be of service, rather than to seek the places of calm and serenity where that vibration of healing will be maintained. This is not an aspect of duality, not an either/or, not a matter of a good or bad choice. It is a matter of being fully and completely open with yourself, your needs and your heart. It is a matter of understanding whether you are a Florence Nightingale or a Gandhi. Both are saints.

"If you are one who has chosen the path of the builder, the seeker of new places, the places of tranquility and rebirth, then we suggest to you that you leave now for the places that have been calling you. Long ago we have spoken of the safe zones. These have not changed. Know that the definition of a safe zone is the place that beckons your heart and speaks to your soul. They are never the places of urban intrigue.

"The issue for those who seek to remain on Earth, and indeed the issue for all is not whether to live amidst chaos or tranquility. The issue is to live in Love and joy. The entire purpose of this existence, and of all existence, is the joining together wholly and inexorably with the heart and soul of the Divine. That is why the opportunity of the Thirteenth Octave has occurred, so that union be felt, experienced, and known by many.

"When we speak to you of the souls passing through the gateway, know that we do not do so in the sense of division. It would be our greatest joy if everyone chose this day, this very moment, to unite totally and completely with us, with All, with God. It is the final unfoldment. It would be our greatest joy to welcome all of you into our loving embrace never to be separated again. If 4,000 or 4 billion choose to walk through this doorway, all will be welcome with equal jubilance. My horn of freedom will sound and the choruses of the heavenly host will indeed sing Hosanna!

"It simply appears at this moment that the gift will only be accepted by a few, but understand that this rather small group, having joined with us, with the Divine, will have the effect of a wildfire out of control. Their Love and heart healing will touch millions upon millions. They are not our chosen ambassadors but our colleagues who walk the Earth, who will be able to walk and teach with Jesus Sananda, James and the Ascended Ones upon their return, which will be shortly. Some will remain in the cities and some will travel to the far-flung outbacks of your planet. The places of desolation and the places of joy will see their presence. In their wisdom they will see and know all situations as One, and all hearts as the reflection of the One Divine Source.

"But we tell those of you who choose the path of the Thirteenth, begin preparation now. There is no time for thoughtful consideration. The blockages must be cleared and the debris swept away. We tell you this now because it will be much harder to complete clearing once the changes have started in earnest. It is better to clear immediately and then go forward in service, than to find yourself struggling to enter later when you will be bombarded by many emotions and experiences which have been deemed by human history as negative.

"So we, the Council of Love conclude this message by thanking all of you who serve, especially those who serve by leaving. Do not fear your passage home, it is a rose strewn path scented with lilac and protected from the wind. You are all loved and cherished dear ones. Go in peace and go in Love. And remember, decide!"

I don't think I will ever forget channeling this next piece. While the tone of our beloved Jesus Sananda was a welcome reprieve it was these words which follow that in fact had the deepest impact on me personally, on my process. His entreaty to love and forgive all aspects of our selves, to integrate and welcome in all parts of our being, struck a deep cord. It was not a cord that I was very familiar with but as I delved into the work He invited and invites us to undertake the transformation was deep – and yes, at times scary. The guidance to love all parts of our being, not only the "devil" but the "saint" was hard. The saint part was much harder because we have all been programmed in one way or another not to think of ourselves that way. When I was growing up it was downright dangerous to think too highly of yourself. Not only was conceit a sin, it was a feeling to me of base self-aggrandizement.

Jesus also speaks in this next article of how many will choose this decision point of entry into he Thirteenth Octave in 2012 – well, we are there.

Trust and Forgiveness: The Keys to Entering the Thirteenth Octave

"Greetings, I am Lord Jesus Sananda. I come this day to speak of trust and forgiveness, to show you by my gentle touch the meaning of healing heart. As I have told you, the gift upon returning from the Thirteenth Octave is the instantaneous healing of another's heart.

"Preparation and decision to move though the energy field into the Thirteenth Octave can raise the most acute feelings of fear and insecurity. Long ago I have told you that the keys to heaven are trust and forgiveness, well now I repeat and say that the keys to the Thirteenth Octave are also trust and forgiveness. The passage you are about to undertake is a leap of faith, a separation from all you have known on this human plane of existence. It would be adequate to raise fear in your heart if we were to ask you to take the giant step of forgiving all those who have caused you injury and grief not only during this lifetime but for all lifetimes and all existences. When that clearing has been completed, the forgiveness we ask you to extend is to self, yes to forgive yourself of all real or imagined grievances, to forgive yourself for all the perceived wrongs and failures you have committed throughout time.

"Part of the process of preparation to enter the Thirteenth Octave is the reintegration of the many denied aspects of self. As you reintegrate all your denied aspects do not deceive yourself, there will be some aspects that you find distasteful, even despicable. That is why you have denied this aspect in the first place, it was uncomfortable, and it caused feelings of chaos within you. It was easier to deny than to accept, alter and change. Now dear ones the time has arrived to put aside those judgments of self/ selves, and having done so to leave this plane behind and enter a new state of being, the Thirteenth Octave.

"Understand you cannot enter a state of wholeness with All That Is and All That Can Ever Be with only a portion of yourself. Also understand that this undertaking has many rewards, the least of which is that you will reintegrate those aspects of self that were perceived as too outstanding, too stellar to maintain. Much of human experience is distrustful and disdainful of both extremes. The human race has come to be fearful of both extremes. This is ironic when one considers the original plan for Earth. The purpose was for pure unadulterated spirit to know joy, to have the experience of being in a physical body while maintaining their angelic knowing and wholeness. With entry into the Thirteenth Octave that purpose is restored and completed.

"There are other issues that also raise fears within your heart at the prospect of entry into the Thirteenth Octave. It is because the invitation requests that you leave all known planes of human existence at this juncture in the unfoldment of the Divine Plan. For some the prospect of leaving all human experience and reality behind is appealing, as there are those who have never adapted well to the human form. But know also that this wishing to leave Earth is a form of denial. Denial that your true spirit, whole and mighty has chosen to enter into this reality and have this experience. That form of denial also must be cleared and eliminated prior to entry into the Thirteenth Octave. Know that this is particularly true for many who will continue along the path of 12:12, that is why they will wait until 2012 to enter the doorway into the Thirteenth Octave. They must first learn what it is to exist wholly and completely within the human form while consciously maintaining their connection to the Divine.

"The invitation to exit the realm of the cycle of 12:12 is assured to raise fears on a cellular level. It speaks to the very core of your being, to the survival mechanism, which is part and parcel of the human equipment. This fear is further magnified by the additional leap of faith which will require you to leave that realm of existence behind while continuing to straddle realities, dimensions and states of being. All the while you continue your path of spirit, and, become a service worker for the rest of humanity; a humanity that will not genuinely have the capacity to comprehend your realm of existence or experience.

"We, the Council of Love, assure you that the rewards are many, and that we will come and walk with you in the new way of being. But accept that inner voice which questions you and demands to know what assurances you have that this will transpire. Understand that fear is the guardian of trust and forgiveness. It alerts your heart and soul that there are blockages that need to be addressed, a small child alone and frightened who needs to be reassured. Think if you were a helpless toddler and you were told that you needed to cross the continent alone to see your parents, to receive loving support. Even if you were offered all assurances that you would be accompanied, escorted, and have every physical and security need addressed, you would still be in a state of trepidation.

"So do not judge your fear, thank it and ask its assistance in more clearly identifying those areas which need to be coddled and taken care of. Understand fear occurs on many levels, from cellular to the most complex system of spiritual existence. You do not wish to extinguish your eternal flame; the fear is that basic and that complex. All you have to go on is trust, but you cannot fully trust until you have forgiven. The cycle of fear, trust, fear is a mechanism to serve you, not defeat you. Accept that built in mechanism, use it and go forward. You are not stuck; you simply are in the cycle of 12:12.

"Throughout your life you have always striven to help others, to understand and forgive those who consciously or unconsciously hurt you. You have tried to live my message of forgiveness and doing unto others. But you have forgotten one essential piece of that teaching, one essential element of that practice. You have forgotten to Love and forgive yourself; to Love and forgive all of yourself. To accept and allow yourself to know not only the wonderful shining star you are but all parts, warts and all. To Love and cherish that thoughtless child, the ignorant fool, the critical cynic, the bitter heartless part of you.

"I am here with you this day of endings and new beginnings to tell you that it is my wish, part of the Divine unfoldment, that you love, forgive and cherish all parts of you. All parts are an extension of the Divine; all parts must be called home, nurtured and loved so they can be made whole. What you deem and despise as the part of your being, which you wish to disown, is the very part of you I ask you this day to forgive, wholly and completely, for all time and throughout eternity.

"Intentions are extremely important, but sometimes intentions and actions go astray. Very often it is how you have learned on the planes of the twelve existences. It is part of the process of human existence. It is how you have come to know me. For I have always come for you in your darkest hours. Never think that I will desert you or will not be present exactly when you have need of me. When many of spoken of me as Savior it meant helper, helpmate.

"The promise I exact from you this day and for all time is to forgive yourself. Allow fear to be released, for there is no fear when you have felt my continued and continual presence and support. Release it. Now. Feel my lightness enter within you, and warm your heart. You are released from the fears and worry which drown you. You are safe; all parts of you are safe and loved, cherished by your guides, this Council of Love and myself. Know this, trust this, and accept this forever. When you are willing and ready, allow yourself to enter my embrace as I take you home, into the Thirteenth Octave, to your life, to your family, to your heart."

Archangel Gabrielle helps us understand the infinite nature of the Universe. There is always something new in the Universe. There is always something new to explore and experience. This new circle of existence has been created by One for all of us, and her horn is beckoning us.

The Thirteenth Octave: A New Circle of Existence

"Greetings from the Council of Love, I am Gabrielle, Lily of Love and Herald of God. We wish to speak this day about the many changes you and those on Earth can anticipate after going and returning to the Thirteenth Octave, the place of wholeness within the Universal Mind and Soul.

"Long ago, I have told the world of my horn of freedom, my trumpet of truth. The purpose of my sound, which is the sound of God, is not to warn or harm or to announce the end of the world, but to announce the arrival of a new way of being, a new hope, a new ray of existence. This new realm of existence will be of benefit to all, not simply those who hear and not simply those who enter the new octave. During each of the initiations I will come and sound my horn at the moment when those present enter the Thirteenth Octave and unite with the heart of the Divine. The union of all those present with the essence of Oneness will be simultaneous. It will similar on the spiritual realm to a nuclear explosion, for the power of so many in human form coming together in wholeness, merging with sheer energy will indeed be worth heralding.

"The sound of my horn will cause a vibration not just in the heart but throughout the entire body of the individuals, and the body of the collective. There will be a merger of a magnitude never felt before on Earth, not even when our beloved Jesus Sananda walked here. The ripple effects will begin to be felt immediately by all on Earth. Of course Jesus will be in attendance for this is His celebration. He is the host. When the sound of God is made it hallmarks a very sacred occasion and the vibration is felt and heard throughout the Universe. Each person present at the initiation will feel and hear the vibration; it is one of the gifts.

For you, it will be your indication and the indication to those present that the undertaking has been completed and successful.

"There will be those who are on a spiritual path who will question how the Thirteenth Octave is different or "new," given that there is nothing new in the Universe. Know right now and feel within your heart that they are completely and utterly wrong. God is a being or energy beyond comprehension to most, even those who have spent many eons of time at His side and within His embrace. This is not because God wishes to remain a mystery being but because He is constantly changing, evolving and inventing new forms, new ways for all to unite with His energy, new ways in which to become One with Him.

"The Universe is not static, it never has been. Nothing remains the same if it is a part of the Divine; it is dynamic; it is living, breathing and having different experiences, continually reaching different levels of knowing. This change is not the same as chaos for it is self-directed in concert with the heart of God. It is expansive in tandem with the Universe, not in combat with it. This is why the Earth has wished to move and evolve beyond her former state of a third dimensional being. She has always understood the bigger picture, the grander scheme.

"Many have believed, and they have been correct, that the purpose of their spiritual journey here on Earth has been to clear all blockages, remove all debris. Then, in that state of balance, they again correctly believed, they are able to join and experience the Divine. This is a state of momentary bliss or ecstasy through concentrated meditation, spiritual practice and a life of clarity. This union with the Divine, particularly for those who do so on a daily basis, results in and promotes a state of balance and extreme joy. To date, that was all that was truly available to those within your energy grid, the gird of twelve planes and twelve existences. Now this has changed.

"God created the next energy plane, the next circle long ago, but it has never been open or available to those on Earth. That is why it initially will be difficult for some to understand and accept. Those in a state of advanced knowing, those who through their daily ritual of joining with the Divine will be the least resistant, for they have always known that there was more beyond the veil. They have always prayed that they would enter the next phase alive, conscious and ready.

"It is those who have pursued a spiritual path and have not yet reached that plateau who will question. It is a good thing that they question, for it opens their hearts and minds to new information. They have trepidation for they are like small children worrying about what will happen if they do not choose, what will happen if they do not enter, what will happen if they do enter, what will happen if they are left behind. These questions, this process, catapult them to where they need to be, to take the next step, and begin earnest preparation to enter the Thirteenth Octave. With the preparation and clearing of outstanding debris they will shed their concerns and cynicism and become enthusiastic about the possibilities of a new creation of an energy field; a new gift from their personal and One Creator to their hearts and their beings. For as we have said before, this is a very personal gift. While there can be group initiations, the gift, the passage, the entry is a soul/sole journey.

"You come together in large groups to merge energy, to increase your vibrations to such a level that you can accept the next levels of energies without blowing your circuits. You come together to celebrate. You come together in groups so that we may reach many at once, to create a group dynamic and synthesis that will be greater than the individual parts. Yes, it would be possible for us to reach the hearts of each person individually, and some will be touched in this way. But it is our method to use larger groups because the purpose of the entry into the Thirteenth Octave is to return in service to the One, and the one united humankind who remains within their path of 12:12. This is a community undertaking with mutual support. Love and unity are the benefits of this type of gathering. Also fun, for believe me when I say the Divine intent of this entire process is Joy, that means having fun!"

During the time when I was channeling this amazing series of articles I was also going through a very painful marital beak-up. As with many, the dissolution of my marriage raised so many heart-rending questions about me, of where I had gone wrong, what I could have done differently, how I had been blind – the list is endless. Which you know if you have ever been through one of those "dark nights." The situation, the sense of failure, of lost dreams, makes you challenge and question your very core, even when you know that you are alright and everything is according to Divine Plan.

This article, "Surrender Unto Wholeness," pulled me back from that abyss, reminded me that we all always carry that God spark within; that we are never less than; and we can never place false gods human or otherwise before us.

Surrender Unto Wholeness

"Greetings from the Council of Love, I am Gabrielle, Lily of Love and Trumpet of Truth. The misconception of most souls upon Earth is that they believe that they have returned to the planet less than whole. There is a common misunderstanding that you are incomplete and that by service and sacrifice you will earn Love and become whole. That is totally erroneous.

"Each being whether on Earth, heaven or throughout the galaxies is one hundred% whole. The Love and sense of wholeness being sought is already within you dear ones. You have always carried the spark, the essence of God within. That Love is what allows you to operate and exist in what is essentially a dense environment. When you seek opportunity to join in Love with another, you do so to seek a complement, a mirror of your own magnificent perfection. You do not do so in order to fill a gap or to complete thy sacred self. You are and always have been complete.

"The opportunity for entry into the Thirteenth Octave is not so much a new opportunity as it is an ancient re-awakening and full anchoring of this realization. There are as many who need to go through this doorway as there are grains of sand on the beach. The belief of lack of wholeness became endemic on your planet when generation after generation came to believe this misunderstanding was actual truth. When you have been instructed in an earlier time not to place false gods above you the meaning was twofold. The first was to not allow any being or life form ascendance over your divine self. The second was to never allow any being that is less than the truth to stand before you.

"The belief system that one is not born on Earth with Love, presently and throughout eternity, is incorrect. This belief became so pervasive that small children, the essence of trust and Love, placed aside their own knowing so as to please their caretakers and parents. Parents similarly placed aside the swell of heart to comply with the demands of ruthless leaders who wished to destroy man and woman on Earth. It was the form of war waged upon Earth during the conflagration of the interplanetary wars. Earth's technology was so primitive that there was no need to destroy the physical being of planet. The plot was much more subtle and horrendous. The implant of false belief systems, which almost destroyed the essence of knowing, was the tactic utilized against the citizens of Earth.

"This movement to destroy, not the inner presence of Love for that can never be eradicated, but the awareness of that Love was the work of what has been known as "dark forces." That conflict has long since been resolved on this side, which is why the denseness now lifts upon your planet; the veil removed; the illusion cracking. It is time for all upon Earth to awaken to the call of my horn. I announce a glorious new day when peace shall reign not for one thousand years but forever. The grid and strands of your DNA were rewoven last year (1996). The new strands do not include the false encoding. Wake up Earth beings; celebrate the new dawn of reawakened Love. Surrender unto wholeness."

Jesus Sananda gave us even more blessings, reminding us of the full anchoring of our soul designs, and how out of despair, comes new beginnings, new opportunities. The Master reminds us once again the key to everything is to love, to love ourselves, everybody on the planet and to simply be Love.

Unconditional Love: The Gift of the Thirteenth Octave and Creation

"Greetings, I am Jesus Sananda, brother and friend, fellow traveler. I come this day to speak to you of unconditional Love – for it is the only kind of Love there is. There are many expressions upon the planet that speak of Love but they do not truly encompass the absence of expectation or conditions. There is a great deal of despair, of disconnection, of disassociation upon the planet at this time and it is the feeling of disconnection from self. This is a feeling of truly not knowing that you are part of All, and not knowing which way to turn. Where you have need to turn my brothers and sisters is inward, deep to the core of your being. I do not speak of the personality that is present in this lifetime but rather of the soul essence, the full design that has been activated within you. It is time for you to become fully familiar with this design and to embrace it and the wholeness of yourself – that is what this creation exercise is about – it is the co-creation as the expression of your design.

"What does this have to do with Love? Where there is feeling of pain, where there is feeling of disappointment, of despair, of disconnection, of hurt, there is no Love. Let me be clear about this. Yes my brothers and sisters I know this feeling for I have walked this Earth as one of you – and many of you have walked with me and you have turned to me and said 'Lord, it has never been this bad, it cannot get any worse.' And then of course it did, and some of you sat and wailed against the enemy and some of you ran away, some of you ended your life, but many of you saw this time of bleakness as new beginning, as opportunity to touch and open the hearts of many. Because where there is despair there is also the deepest yearning to be and to exist in Love – otherwise there would not be this feeling of desolation – there would simply be a feeling of nothing but emptiness.

"You look around your planet and see the chaos blossoming from those who would take up arms and destroy your brothers and sisters, to those who simply sit in depression, to those who are leaving the planet by the millions. Once again you say to me

'Lord it has never been so bad; how can you speak of new beginnings and Nova Earth and the fullness of the unfoldment of the plan of the Divine Mother when all we see is darkness. What can we do?' And I say to you, love yourself. For if you are not wholly and completely, unconditionally in acceptance and Love of yourself there is no resolution, no Light. There needs to be a complete embracing of who you are. This does not mean acceptance or lack of responsibility. It does not mean to say to yourself 'Oh, I have behaved badly but it is OK because I love myself.' No, it is to look at the dark spots within you and say I will love myself, I will change this, and I will shift the energy to an absolute reflection of Love. And how will you do this? You will do it by the actions of Love – trust, hope and forgivingness. The expression of this is not just to love those who are similar to you but also to love your enemies and those you distain; to love those you think are insane. It is to take them into your heart with compassion and wholeness and to hold them close to you, the same way you would hold a child who is throwing a tantrum and is out of control. You will hold them so that they will not harm themselves or anyone else. That is what has need to transpire – not to drop into the depths of despair; for out of the darkness is the Light.

"Understand my brothers and sisters, as above so below. In the existence in the heart of God, in the Universe, in the heart of One, there is only Love – there is nothing else. It is when you move to this point, the connection of unity that you are home. We bring you home, home to the heart of Mother/Father that you may hold and exist in this Oneness and then express it upon the planet. That is the gift of the Thirteenth Octave – it was to instantaneously heal the hearts of everyone on the planet. It was a gift prematurely given and never before bestowed - to be able to be in physical form and simultaneously connected to the heart of One.

"Make this connection deeper; forge this connection to Love more solidly than you ever have before. Where you are feeling despair, pain, disconnection, love it away. No, I do not mean acceptance of it; I mean complete and total surrender. For it is a myth, an illusion, it is part of the mindset of mankind that has created separation.

"I have known moments of despair and I have known moments of human love, and in this day and in this moment I know my complete Love for you – for each and every one of you – not just as a spirit you are but for every hair on your head, every smile, every pore on your skin, every action you take, you are Loved. So when you do not know how to proceed, when you feel limited, turn to me and say to me 'Lord, how will I Love myself?' And then let me show you.

"We walk the planet together during this time of momentous change, opportunity and yes my friend challenges like you have never known on Earth before. But let me clear – I have come to walk with you, hand in hand. So I would dearly hope you would not leave and I would dearly hope and trust that you will not turn your head away and absorb the negativity, despair and chaos that are now departing the planet. The chaos has need to ascend, as that is truly the meaning of the Ascension! It is the Ascension of all former emotional beings into new form, into clarity and light.

"You have hesitated to proceed with your creations and the hesitation has come from the lack of acknowledgement and Love of self so what I ask of you now, your next assignment, is to take time every single day and preferably every single hour to check in with me and to see that you are Love, nothing but Love. That is your soul design; it is the expression of Love. You took the best you thought of the Father, the most glorious expression and you said, 'OK, I will go exploring now, for I have my suitcase packed – it is called my soul design.' You are prepared, you have all you need, you are my disciples, my apostles of Nova Earth. Come walk with me now. Farewell."

This channeling by Archangel Gabrielle was given to us during the initiation into the Violet Flame Temple of St. Germaine. It is a powerful reminder that regardless of how far we travel or how much we learn, that when we really need to detach and heal, all we need to do is go home. Go home, curl up in the arms of the Mother/Father and allow ourselves to be restored.

Stay in the Thirteenth Octave and Heal

"Greetings I am Gabrielle, Ruler of Love and Trumpet of Truth, Messenger of One. Welcome dear children. Welcome to this temple and welcome to this circle, welcome home. I come to continue to speak to you of being and staying healthy, of being whole and being one with One.

"It is time for you and the unfoldment of your perfect soul design to know of the wholeness of your being, and the wholeness and enjoyment of your physical body. We have told you when you have asked why you do not heal and why you do not seem capable of healing your physical self, to come home, to come home to the Thirteenth Octave and stay there. Many of you have forgotten and some of you have never known what the Thirteenth Octave is and hence we tell you again, it is the heart of One. It is the body, mind, spirit, will, and Love of what you think of as God. It is beyond physicality; it is far beyond what you think of within the available realm of twelve planes and twelve dimensions, the twelve levels of existence. It is a state of being in which you are All; it is a closing of the circle to go home, beyond any existence, any lifetime, any reality, any Universe, it is to simply be with One.

"There are many things during this time of integration and change that we wish to share with you, to remind you of. Think of it in exactly the same way as when you have gone to a parent, or grandparent or a friend and sat and listened to the story about who you are, about your family, about how things have been and how they can be. It is not simply the stories that we wish you to hear; it is not simply the messages of Love, the words, which are so primitive. It is the receiving of the energy of Love into your heart and very being. When you are fully anchored in this energy there can be no illness, no disease, no war, no pain, and no despair."

This final piece is from Jesus Sananda and once again He is inviting us to join him in the Thirteenth Octave. He explains this gift in terms of our Ascension process – it will make our transition smooth, graceful and complete. How could we possibly say no – why would we want to?

An Update on the Thirteenth Octave – January 13, 2012

"Greetings I am Jesus Sananda. Welcome seekers of the Light. Welcome to this time of awakening, of Ascension and entering into a reality of inter-dimensional potential and creation. Long ago I have beckoned to you to come and join me in the heart of One. I have asked each of you to come and reunite in the heart of One – in the Thirteenth Octave. So many of you have and for this all of us on this side are eternally and infinitely grateful.

"I speak to you this day about the Thirteenth Octave in terms of Ascension – both for you personally, and, in terms of the Shift that your beloved Gaia now goes through. The entry to the Thirteenth Octave was opened by the Mother/Father/One in order to prepare for this time that is now at hand. You had need to learn that you are not only Love but that you are united in heart with All That Is – not only with this company of heaven but your star brothers and sisters, the human collective, the galaxies, the grass, trees, elementals and yes, Gaia. You have come to mentally understand this but your heart still needs greater expansion and that is why once again we extend this heartfelt invitation for each of you to join us in the Thirteenth Octave.

"Many of you say 'why Lord do you ask us to do this when we are already in the process of Ascension and change?' I beseech you because of this Ascension process. When you unite in the heart of One you have transcended all dimensions of the human reality and experience. From there you are free to travel to the seventh, the fifth, the ninth or wherever you choose. When you come and join with us in the heart of Love you then float down gently and softly into the reality you wish to occupy. This is by far more effective and possible than trying to climb out of the density of the third dimension through the fourth and hopefully landing in the fifth. When you come home to the Thirteenth you then return immediately as a gatekeeper and extend your energies and being to those who are attempting to make this transition.

"The plan of the Universal Mother does not require struggle – we have created the gentlest, most loving way for you to accompany Gaia in this transition. So once again we invite you home to the heart of All – we invite you home to the heart of creation. Your journey, your choice of this incarnation is not to remain on this side but rather to return and complete this trans-dimensional Shift as way-showers, as pathfinders, as teachers and channels, as emissaries from the heart of One. You knew fully that this opening would be made available to you, perhaps years ahead, and for some of you at the last moment. It matters not – the choice is yours, and the door is open.

"Come travel with me to the Thirteenth and then accompany all of us who return to walk the Earth in peace and harmony – walk with us in the fifth, the sixth, the seventh – for this is where Gaia will be anchored.

"Time as you know it is short my beloved ones. Do not tarry. The gifts of the Thirteenth Octave are yours to claim, and they will assist you enormously in this final task at hand. Archangel Gabrielle, Universal Mother Mary, Yahweh, Michael, Sanat Kumara – all of us call to you. Listen to your heart and then proceed bravely – we are here to shepherd you through. Go in peace and go with our Love. Farewell."

• Listen to the "Thirteenth Octave" audio file to complete your initiation into the Thirteenth Octave.

Entry into the Thirteenth Octave changes everything. It alters how you think, feel, process and behave. It has been an amazing adventure over the years to share and observe how initiates have transformed. Repeatedly I would hear, "well nothing happened during the meditation – well except when Jesus came in, or Archangel Michael, or Universal Mother." We'd then laugh, realizing the enormity of the experience.

Some people have incredible experiences, and some none at all, but in the ensuing weeks they report their way of being has subtly but remarkably shifted. Things that used to be triggers, old issues, old hurts, are simply gone. New abilities or the realization of dearly held dreams begin to take shape.

A significant change is that in the early years the changes would be slow and very subtle, gentle. Now the shift occurs instantaneously. There's no waiting to see if you made it, because we all do. The knowing is beyond question, undeniable.

It seems unfathomable that any being would not take full advantage of this precious gift, of the transmutation and transformation it offers. Share this process and gift with everyone you meet, share it with your loved ones, strangers, and the guys down the street. Because, this is part of our collective Ascension process. This is our jumping off point. This is why we came.

Chapter 3

The Thirteenth Octave
Blessings & Virtues

As we shift with our beloved Gaia from the third to the fifth dimension, and perhaps higher, what we are doing is creating, constructing, and building Nova Earth, Nova Society – new ways of being in human connectedness, unity and balance. We are not arriving in the fifth dimension with everything in place and ready for us like a five-star hotel – this is a process of co-creation of not only above and below but with Gaia, with the kingdoms, with the elementals and devas, with our star brothers and sisters.

In 2000, we began anchoring and receiving information about the Wingmakers (our future selves) and the Cities of Light. Since that time many of us have been involved in anchoring Cities of Light all over the planet, and vigorously in North America. This process has been to first open and anchor a portal and then begin the anchoring of these magnificent cities. Each of these cities has a different function – some for healing (North Carolina), some as star being portals (Idaho), some for beauty and art (New Orleans). The first City of Light to be anchored was the Phoenix/Sedona City of Light which is known as the New Jerusalem. But the list is long, exciting and growing rapidly.

We have witnessed and battled in the past few years with the elimination and disintegration of the paradigms of Old Earth. The belief systems that have been created and based on human creations at the lowest end of the vibratory scale. The major old paradigms, also known as false grids, are

L – lack, limitation, loss – this includes abandonment, isolation, loneliness and lack of self-worth and self-Love, and self-doubt

D – death, destruction, disease, despair, disbelief – this ability to never believe – lack of faith and trust; depression, disgust

F – fault, blame, anger, fear, self-doubt and denigration can also appear here

G – greed, lust, control – includes abuse of power, jealousy and mercenary or stingy belief and behaviors belong here

C – cruelty; think of people who have many lives in war or torture

E – ego; as in royalty, excess, exclusion

F – failure (this can also be related and found in the fear - but here the COL means a belief system that nothing ever works - failure is inevitable

H – hatred, harm and hubris (inappropriate pride and narcissism belongs here)

Almost anything you can imagine can be a false grid – once you start working with them you will see.

Now about repair. Once you have identified the false grid think, feel, sense and listen to what needs to be replaced from the twelve dimensions and planes to fill that gap, and gather it within. After a while it becomes natural. In the last year the elimination of false grids has been a consistent theme in my channeling work both with individuals and groups. People are being instilled with grace, joy, confidence and forgiveness. But the key is to go with the blessing and virtue that comes up for you – that will be the key to fill what you are letting go of and clearing once and for all. If you are experiencing difficulty in any form of clearing, I encourage you to use Universal Mother Mary's gift of removal – one of the original gifts of the Thirteenth Octave. You can't go wrong with this – it takes but a minute. I know lots of folks who do this in their car, in the washroom, at work, at home – whenever something comes up that is not of Love; that does not feel like the wholeness and connection you claim as you birthright, give it Mary. I know personally that it heals everything from a broken heart to depression, disease, and at the same time opens your heart to miracles and the true practice of receiving.

Universal Mother Mary's Removal Exercise

"Within the heart of each of you there rests the seed of sorrow, the grief of humanity, the pain of this Mother Earth. Place your right hand upon your heart and cover it with your left and feel the seed of the past be placed upon your palm. Allow it to be removed from the self, from the soul; take your hands and arms in spiral and to give it to me. You may, and can, always bring your troubles to your Universal Mother, and I will take them from you. I place upon your hands the full recognition of the beauty of your essence. To bring back within your being, place your left hand upon your heart so as to instill it with me. I wish my home, this planet, to be filled with laughter, dreams and play. Remember, you are my children. Even as angels you must frolic and rejoice in all the glory that you are. I attend to you and your needs, great and small. So keep me close little ones."

This precious gift from our Universal Mother Mary allow us to remove all pain, grief and suffering from our hearts and to receive in replacement, that which we pray and yearn for. It helps us become our full self as vehicles for the path of service. Once we understand how to use the gift, we may share it with others and undertake to do this exercise on behalf of others, including large groups. This means we have been given a gift to heal and inspire the world. This gift is extremely powerful and a potent reminder of the importance of prayer and intent.

How to:

Take your right hand and gently lay it upon your heart. Place your left hand on top of your right. Close your eyes. Feel that which is burdening you deep within your heart and say a little prayer or invocation to Mother Mary. Request her help to remove this burden. Feel the energy begin to flow from your heart into the center of the right palm. Really feel it penetrate – perhaps you will feel warmth or tingling. When you feel the heart expansion and a readiness to let go (yes, you'll know) take your hands and roll them out, hand over hand, until your arms are extended directly in front of you. Make sure your palms are facing up; similar to the position you have seen Mary in many paintings.

You will begin to feel a tingling in the tips of your fingers. The sensation is the same for everyone, so pay attention and accept no substitutions. This tingling is Mary removing this burden.

When this stops, keep your hands extended outward, palms up and ask from your heart for that which you wish to receive. If you are uncertain what to ask for because all you're doing is concentrating on receiving relief, ask Mary to send you that which is for your highest good and the highest good for all concerned. Another way is to focus on the opposite of what you have just let go. For example, if you let go of grief, then call for joy. If it is anger, call for calm. Ask Mary with all your heart to grant this to you today – at that moment. Feel the heaviness in the center of both palms. Feel your palms get heavier and heavier until it is a struggle to hold your arms up. The gifts of the Universal Mother are many and can weigh a lot. Proceed to roll your hands back in towards your heart, left hand first. Place you left hand upon your heart and feel the gift you have just received penetrate your heart right to its core. Feel the gentle smile within.

Finish, as always, for all sacred ceremonies, with a prayer. Thank Mary for the gift, her guidance and her Love.

When you have this down pat, it takes about thirty seconds. Remember the keys to this exercise are intent, prayer, the physical action and then thanksgiving. Don't neglect the physical action for it is this message to the Universe that brings the gift into the physical reality of your body and the world.

When conducting this exercise on behalf of another, or for a group, follow the same process but become the vehicle for them. For example, if you were removing the pain of all the families caught in the terror of a hurricane, you would feel that in your heart, give it away and receive from Mary peace, tranquility, courage and physical strength. If you were doing it for those who are sick or dying, you would remove pain, sense of loss, despair and anger. In their stead, you would receive Love, serenity and knowing the Love of God.

Now back to the thirteen Blessings and Virtues. What are the values that we choose to be the inherent basis of everything we create? When I began questioning the inclusion of this in our Ascension process Archangel Gabrielle in all her might and glory became very insistent. With Sanat Kumara, keeper of Universal Law and Planetary Logos at her side, I didn't stand a chance. "Child you are seeing the illusion of the old paradigms of Earth; the elimination of lack, limitation, control, greed, death, destruction, disease – but what would you have replace this? What is the new foundation upon which Nova Earth is built? It is the thirteen Blessings and Virtues that we gifted you so long ago. This is the core of everything you will value and bring forth in the new reality. This is the foundation of what you create and co-create with us. If the virtues are not an inherent part of your being, how do you then translate it into form as you build the new institutions, systems, communities, and cultures of Nova Earth?"

The ceremony and process of receiving and anchoring the thirteen Blessings and Virtues is sacred but can also be a heck of a lot of fun. When I facilitate a Thirteenth Octave workshop we have an exercise that we do where small groups of two or three choose a blessing and then perform it. We have had everything from belly dancing to kittens. This is something you can do with friends or create an actual or virtual ceremony for yourself. By virtual I mean that there are so many incredible photographs on the internet that you can surf and find what speaks to your heart as representative of your virtue. Making it physical is great in any situation for truly anchoring the energy into your body.

The Ceremony and Process

"Greetings from the Council of Love on this day of renewed hope and faith. This is James the Apostle of our Lord Jesus Christ, Savior, Son of Yahweh.

"Know that when we speak of the concept of Blessings and Virtues that the terms are interchangeable. If one has a virtue it is indeed a blessing not only to the individual but to the whole. While there are many, many Blessings and Virtues, which are available throughout the Universe, we speak this day of the core virtues necessary to go forward without blockages or debris. It allows one to maintain a state of wholeness.

"The instilling of the thirteen Blessings and Virtues is one of the most important gifts received during the initiation and attunement to the Thirteenth Octave. The virtues and blessings have been very specifically chosen by the Council of Love from amongst a host of blessings. This grouping of Blessings and Virtues is intended to equip you with those qualities necessary to complete your mission of service to others. Each carries a distinct vibration that will become irrevocably a part of your being during the initiation process.

"The Council directs the ceremony relating to the bestowing of the Blessings and Virtues be as interactive as possible, and, has given specific instructions regarding preparation as well as the ceremony itself. So please read, consider and meditate on the following information. It is intended to assist you in clearing and readying yourself to receive these gifts.

"First, breathe, inhale and cover yourself with the silver ray seven times. Then read the following information and incorporate it into your place of knowing within your heart. During your daily meditation take time to feel each of the virtues individually. Work with each virtue, including the color and ray. Notice and make note of sounds, scents and impressions of each. It can be helpful to keep a journal of your observations. The information will be helpful not only to yourself but others if you choose to do this with friends. Notice the different vibration of each, where it sits within your physical body, how it makes you feel, your reaction, especially any resistance to incorporating that virtue into your life.

"After you have worked and experienced each blessing and virtue you are ready for the next step, which is to select a virtue you wish to align with and represent during your personal ceremony. Let me further explain. Each of you will be instilled with all the thirteen Blessings and Virtues, but as mentioned earlier, the Council requests the process to be interactive where possible and realistic.

"In selecting the blessing and virtue with which you wish to align, it is not a matter of first instinct being correct. It is natural for most of you to gravitate towards those aspects that immediately make life more enjoyable, such as joy or beauty. Go deeper. The selection of your virtue needs to be made in conjunction with the larger questions of why you choose to enter into the Thirteenth Octave, what you intend to bring back, and what you intend to accomplish with the Divine state of Wholeness. Select the virtue that you feel you will most need in order to accomplish your mission of spiritual service to others. Select the virtue that you feel will assist you most in your Ascension.

"This examination requires that you delve deeply within, to look at that part of yourself that perhaps you feel is lacking. This is why we tell you to examine and re-examine those virtues to which you feel resistance or less than a positive connection. Feel from the deepest part of you that which is either your essence or that which you believe is absent. It can be either because ultimately they are one and the same. That is the virtue to select.

"After you have made your selection, go back into meditation and feel the vibration of that virtue once again. It will feel markedly different. You will know within the core of your being that you have already begun to shift and incorporate as you prepare. When this occurs, do nothing further. Congratulate yourself, you are ready! If you feel nothing, we urge you to go deeper and/or select another virtue – you are not yet there.

"Understand that all of the thirteen Blessings and Virtues are related and reflective of Love, trust and forgiveness, unity, connectedness and balance."

Take your time when reading each of the Blessings and Virtues. Allow yourself to sit with one or two and absorb the energy. Come back to them as you work your way through this Ascension process. And most of all, dear reader, enjoy them – they are a gift to your heart.

The Thirteen Blessings and Virtues

1. Prudence

Twin of temperance. The ability to know in all situations when to proceed and when to retreat; when to take action and when to be still; when to offer help and when to keep silent; to know in exact measure what is required whether it is in baking a cake or healing a psychic injury. All things in correct measure. Prudence encompasses the quality of moderation, the genuine knowing and practice of everything in balance. No one person can live in only one area of their being, their life, and truly be representative of the whole. Prudence allows for the complete and total release of addictions. An unusual trait on Earth. The colors are halion and siroun, which are rays of the higher dimensions and explained below.

Halion is one of the thirteen rays. It is one of the new rainbow rays and is a combination of blue, pink, mauve, some turquoise and violet shot through with mint green. As a chakra it sits at the base of your rib cage and is used as a portal to connect with your star brothers and sisters, as well as to come to know your own star self. Halion was also a planet millions of years ago which evolved to sheer energy. Form was released and the energies of the planet and the collective assumed a new or expanded soul purpose. This energy is known as the halion engineers, constructers – architects – builders of new pure realities be it a building, society or institution. The Council tells us that many of the halion engineers will be assisting us with the building of Nova Earth.

Siroun is the color and ray of peach – soft oranges, pinks, gold; the skin of a peach and the color of a magnificent sunset. As a chakra the siroun sits at the high heart or thymus and is the center for peace, harmony and gentle Love.

2. Fortitude

Courage in all forms, endurance, the ability to keep going forward when others cease and give up. The virtue of path-finders. Strength of purpose. Stamina in all senses. Know that patience is a part of fortitude. Fortitude is the encompassing of forbearance, and forbearance is indeed a quality that requires patience. To continue going forward with stamina when you really feel like pushing the individual off the cliff; it will be required in working with 12:12. The vibration is orange.

3. Hope

The gift of heart-knowing of the presence of God. The ability to understand that very often things on Earth are not as they appear. An ability to pierce the illusion of the veil. The only reason for change. Hope encompasses serenity; total and perfect calm. To be in the world but not of it, to be able to remain centered and still, one with who you are regardless of externals. Hope is the color of deep twilight blue, almost navy. It is the deepest color of blue, the color of our beloved Divine Mother Mary.

4. Purity

Twin of clarity; sister of chastity, not in the sexual sense but in the sense of the ability to remain pure in all aspects of self. To remain centered when there is chaos, temptation or a lack of harmony around you. To see, feel and know clearly what exists, what is illusion and what is necessary for survival in all senses of the word. It is the color of pearlescent white, the color of infants before they ground in their body. It is what all should strive for. It is what you all miss.

5. Beauty

Inner and outer. To be in a state of beauty with all that is, in all realms, physical, emotional and spiritual. The ability to create and maintain beauty. To be in a state of beauty is to be in harmony with all. To become a perfect mirror for all of God's creations. It is two separate colors, silver and magenta.

6. Joy

To be fully thankful, grateful and one with the gift of life purpose and spirit. To be a reflection of the perfection of the creation of self and all. To live in and remain with the heart for all time. Joy is the color of gold.

7. Compassion

The ability to Love and serve without judgment. To be able to fully understand and heart feel another's situation without entering or assuming that cloak. The understanding that another has a chosen path and that we can only offer assistance and Love. We cannot complete another's journey for them for that would be theft. Tenderness. Its colors are green and red.

8. Truth

Truth is clarity. Truth simply is light and Love. It is the wholeness of knowing. It is factual information that can stand and does stand alone, whether people know it or not, truth is. For example, the Divine is a supreme knowing. Whether anyone in this room or on this planet knows this matters not. That truth cannot be altered. Wisdom is the virtue of having the good sense to know and understand that truth. Truth is the color of silver, with tinges of pink and lilac.

9. Wisdom

Brother of Truth. Understanding the Divine plan, the unfoldment and each thing/being's place within that plan. Ultimate respect for all because all is a reflection of the One, and we are One. The ability to comprehend the difference between believing, thinking and knowing. Knowing comes from the deepest core of your being, it is that part of you intimately connected with your higher self, your guides and God. It is the beauty of the elders, of those who have gone through the planes of twelve existences, those who have arrived at the end of the path and are ready for a new time. Wisdom is the dark color of claret.

10. Awe

Ability to feel and experience always and fully the wonders of creation, the Divine. The knowing that there is always more, more to learn, to experience, and to understand. To know that our understanding and experience of God is limited but the promise of further growth holds true. It is the innocence of the small child within, the sense of awe, the sense of wonder. It is the sense of understanding the magnificence of the universal plan, the unfoldment. It is the thrill, the expectation and joy at being, simply being, and enjoying the new miracles that unfold, always waiting for the next one. It is the relation of purity. It is the color of golden saffron.

11. Charity

The genuine ability to share all things, material, spiritual and emotional. Based in the true understanding that there is always enough for all to thrive and we are all richer in the joint expression of sharing. A heart-felt need to be generous. Knowing knowledge and gifts are never intended solely for one person. The vibration is green.

12. Humility

Twin of piety. Ability to be truly grateful of the many blessings bestowed upon each and all. Knowledge that alone we are rather incompetent but united with One we are All. Necessary for all works and sharing of service. Its color is red.

13. Grace

Your final virtue and blessing, grace is the quality of being a true and exact expression of Divine spirit and will. This is a state of beauty, of wholeness, of oneness. It is the final blessing and virtue, encompassing service and action. It is the color of pink.

The thirteen Blessings and Virtues are not simply "feel good" gifts, something to make us feel whole and pure, although they certainly accomplish that as well. They are the foundation upon which we build and conduct our daily lives. Years ago I had a student Will whom I only saw every year and then sporadically. He was deeply committed to his spiritual path and much to my delight every time I saw him his light shone brighter and brighter. Then I didn't see him for a long time, which was good news because he no longer needed me to be the go-between for guidance. But as luck would have it, one day we had a chance to connect on the phone. In discussing his journey and how things were going he shared with me that his practice had been to take one blessing and virtue per month and to really consciously work with it, day in and day out. He'd been doing it for years – and it had worked miracles for him. It had enriched his marriage, deepened his compassion for himself and others, and generally brightened up and expanded his world.

There are periods when I completely blank on the Blessings and Virtues, and then something happens to bring them front and center again, reminding me of the profound nature of this gift.

If you establish a pattern where you take one of the blessings for a day, a week or a month and truly incorporate your behavior and actions accordingly you will be amazed at the shift.

Chapter 4

The Gift of the Violet Flame

When I first encountered St. Germaine I didn't like him. I felt he was brash, arrogant and a little too pushy for my liking. He pushed his way into my consciousness and demanded that I cooperate with being the transmitter for his messages to the world. Unlike my feelings of awe, incredible Love and honoring that I experienced with Jesus, the Universal Mother or Archangel Gabrielle, this Master was way too human for me. Too similar to the personalities I had met during my health care career; so sure of their entitled position in the world. And besides which St. Germaine was pushing me to undertake something that I was extremely uncomfortable with – to expand my horizons and address the arena of healing, and I didn't even know the guy! Didn't he understand that my forte was channeling – how dare he suggest I expand and Shift. Talk about judgment!

When I would cautiously mention this master of the Violet Flame to friends and fellow Lightholders they would light up and say with a uniformity that was scary "Oh, I Love St. Germaine, I've studied his teachings for years. Did you know he was Columbus, Francis Bacon, Shakespeare, and Benjamin Franklin? He's so handsome"… ick! All I was hearing was about his incredible history and the enormous respect this bothersome Master held in people's hearts – and I would probably have to study his works – like I don't have enough to do.

It's laughable now, actually hilarious, as I run to meet this truly beloved Master whose picture and energy sit high about my office door and who guides me every day with such sensitive insight, understanding and Love. That's why I share this with you – to share the laughter but also to say we don't always know what lies ahead and sometimes our human resistance is just our egos blocking what might be a huge gift and the next biggest step in our spiritual journey. It certainly has been for me with St. Germaine. But, as always, he is gently pushing me aside because he wants to make his own introduction to each of you.

But before he does I want to explain about his name and the mysterious extra "e." When I met St. Germaine, I didn't know how to spell his name so when it was channeled St. Germaine with an "e" on the end I didn't question it. Many St. Germaine fans did and the cards and comments correcting my error came flooding in. With the best intentions people explained to me that St. Germaine was spelled St. Germain. To this day, I still receive helpful emails from those who just want me to get it right. I have certainly tried to spell it without the "e", even as the editing for this book began. But always it's been a fruitless exercise, on orders from this unconventional Ascended Master. St. Germaine explains that he wants all of us to understand that his essence, like ours, has expanded. Jokingly, he first told me he added the "e" for excellence. Then he explained that the "e" is to soften the name, to add the element of the Divine Feminine to the very masculine name and energy he is known by. Personally, I think the "e" stands for energy. I honor that request and step aside for our beloved St. Germaine, with an "e."

"Good morning, I am St. Germaine, Master and Keeper of the Violet Flame and the I AM presence. I wake this channel at four-forty a.m. so that I may speak to you, to your hearts in the silence of the early morning; that I may be the one to watch the creeping dawn with you. I do not simply refer to the miracle of the sun rising every day but to the creeping dawn of humanity and of each of you my sweet beloved friends. It is a time of awakening, of stretching and welcoming the new world.

"For many years I have referred to myself as the Keeper of the Violet Flame because I wished to teach you humility and that nothing that is of the collective Source is ever owned or controlled by anyone, above or below. But now you break through the shackles of the third dimension illusions and you begin to see with your heart and not simply your eyes or ego. Therefore you understand the title of Master as an endearment and as a reference to the holy mission I have accepted throughout time and space, throughout eternity.

"I come this day to speak to you of Ascension – of that delightful movement up to the next step of collective evolution in tandem and harmony with Gaia and All That Is. Let me begin by saying my dear friends that you are ready. Please immediately stop all this back and forth movement; this fidgeting of whether you are ready or not, whether you will make it or not. It is an inane conversation with your ego and it is one that bars you from the full reality and potential of who you are. And besides which, I ask you, how does one decide if one is ready for enlightenment? You may study, meditate, pray and follow all the spiritual precepts set forth to you in great abundance by the spiritual hierarchy – but so what. Enlightenment is a gift.

"Ascension is a gift and part of your journey to enlightment. Yes, you are doing your part in making sure you are dressed and ready for the party, that you will be present in every way – that you will show up. But beyond that dear heart – where does fear and uncertainty come in? There is not place for it.

"This Council, the Council of Love of which I am pleased to be a part of (as are you), has given you all the tools you need to accomplish this Shift smoothly and glamorously. Yes, glamorously – arriving in dazzling style – in your unique invincible style. Of course you must embrace that glory and admit to yourself that you have done your work, that you have done the best you can, and that you are not only ready but eager to ascend – to move onward and upward. Yes I know this channel does not like the hierarchical references but this is my channel not hers." (I can hear him laughing).

"In the following excerpts that you are about to read the only thing that is important is that I am speaking to your heart. The words communicate information about who you are and your role as teacher, healer, transmitter, gatekeeper but the true content of these channelings is my working with you, yes even through these electronic words, to fill you with the power and light of the Violet Flame. To reassure you and raise you up, to ready you for lift-off. To be with you, by your side every step of the way in this Ascension process. Why? Because I want to be there with you when you arrive, when you finally see and feel the full impact of the fifth and seventh dimensions. I want to be with you when you sigh and say 'thank God, I'm home.' I want to be with you when you remember our dear friendship and how I Love you. I want to be with you because that is the fulfillment of my promise to each of you long ago. I want to be with you because it will be fun and I am never one to miss out on fun.

"So place your concerns in my violet bonfire – torch each and every one of those shadows of doubt and join with me in this Ascension process. I promise you it will be easy, it will be delightful, and my dearest heart, it will most certainly be worth it.

"I end with a little joke and riddle, which of course always drives the channel wild, but I wish to share this with you. The space shuttle program has not been cancelled, indeed it has just begun. Go in laughter, confidence and please wear purple. Farewell."

There is a plethora of information the Council of Love, the archangels, and the Ascended Masters have channeled on each of the sacred flames as they have bestowed them upon us. Each sacred flame, associated with an ascended one and each particular ray holds numerous gifts, blessings and uses, primarily for healing including clearing, enlightenment, creation and yes, Ascension.

The energy of the Violet Flame, like everything else in this time of intensified energy, has transmuted and grown, as we have morphed enough to handle more. In preparation for sailing smoothly through the Shift the Council of Love invites you to receive this attunement to the Violet Flame and the I AM Presence which helps us raise our frequencies to a place where we are in harmony with all of creation. So that we thrive not merely survive.

The Council never ceases to surprise me; nor do my fellow travelers. However, I was taken aback when the Council's guidance for our opening meditation on the Ascension process at the annual Gathering in Sedona in October 2011 was a clearing exercise. And here I thought we were done with that. My reason for mentioning this is that the Violet Flame of St. Germaine is not only an incredible healing tool but a clearing tool as well. The Violet Flame transmutes, burns away and transforms into wholeness, any debris or obstacles that you need to let go of in order to ascend. And whether we like it or not, let's face it, we still are living in that trans-dimensional reality where 'stuff' comes up and we need, one more time, to let it go.

The Violet Flame of St. Germaine and the I AM presence is imbedded in the tips of each of our fingertips, the center of the palms of both of our hands, our heart, third eye and crown chakra. The flames are ignited by intent and invocation of St. Germaine and can literally be used to "torch" anything. Contact with the Violet Flame transmutes even the most stubborn issue into ashes so that you can rise again like the phoenix, strong, free and with clear vision.

We begin this section with several messages from St. Germaine on the meaning and purpose of his gift of the Violet Flame and then proceed to discussion on how this relates to your Ascension process, your role as gatekeeper and healer of Gaia, and then on to the initiation.

"Greetings, I am St. Germaine, keeper of the Violet Flame, keeper of the I AM presence. I come to you as an ancient friend, teacher, and healer. I sit with you during this time to help you recall, bringing forward what you have always known, to help you assist in the healing of others and this planet. I want to remind you that this gift of the Violet Flame is not something, my beloved friends that you need to acquire. It is something that I have given you long ago, something that has been imbedded within you and that you have carried with you since the time of Atlantis.

"Each of you has gone through many dark nights and many

dark days, dark times when you thought the light would never shine again. But you persisted, and now this time is upon you that you the brave ones incarnate and walk this sacred Earth. This world is filled with wonder, but also with confusion and hatred and greed; gentleness and Love. I walked the world for hundreds and thousands of years waiting for this time when the plan would be resurrected, dusted off and brought out not just to be shown but to be implemented.

"Now, I work with you from this side. I give you my tools and I give you my very essence, the Violet Flame. It is not simply a handy tool that you can use when you feel like it; it is my essence, the power of alchemy, healing and immortality that I give you. These are the gifts being brought forward. You are my torch bearers. You wear my amulet and you carry the truth and the knowing of healing within your heart. I wish you to reignite these flames that I have imbedded within you, within your hands and your fingers, in your heart and your third eye. I wish these to be reignited today and to stay reignited to burn brightly as the message and the reminder that you are also the I AM.

"This is not something you are endeavoring to become; it is something you have always been, that you carry within you, deep within you. Do not hide it, that is false modesty, false humility, and there is no room for it, not during this time of rapid change. You step forward each in your own way to heal the collective. This is done with genuine humility, with an honoring of the sacred self, with an honoring and an understanding of the privilege that is bestowed upon you. This is not a burden, this is an honor and it is an honor that you have claimed for yourself. Is it easy? No. Is it worth it? Yes.

"The day will come when we will sit together again and break bread and share our stories of victory. It is not about being flamboyant, as I have often been accused of being. It is about being clear and not hiding behind a smoke screen. You have not only my support, but the support of millions and millions - you have no idea. You are fortified in unimaginable ways. If you choose to take advantage of this, and why would you not, then there is nothing, nothing that you cannot accomplish. From the anchoring of Cities of Light, to the opening of portals, to the creation of Nova Beings, you have come to see, to witness, to participate, and to lead the fulfillment of the promise. So, do so.

"Show your fellow humans the way; show them the mirror of who they truly are. I do not ask for my essence in any way ever to overshadow you, none of us do because that would be dishonoring of your sacred being which is mighty. But, let us participate, let us help, and let us fortify. I do not walk the Earth, I will not walk the Earth ever again, but that does not mean that my Love for the Earth and for all of you is not present. It is always and ever present.

"You are my armada of healers. And this armada is not founded in the mediocre. It is founded in the strength and truth and the ability to stand and truly be counted, not by denying and side-stepping; it is being your true, peaceful warrior, the warriors of healing. That is why I use this term armada. You're the ones that have venture out. You are the ones who have agreed and taken this mantle of responsibility. For this I thank you, we thank you, and we will never, ever let you down. Let us help. Go in peace."

The Power of the Violet Flame

We have felt the penetration of the sacred essence of the Universal Mother and the enormous expansion of energy over the past year. The theme of many of my client's individual channeling sessions is that people are feeling they have been pushed to the edge of meltdown. There is a pervasive feeling of not knowing if they can go on, because with that expansion has come the often dramatic clearing and rebuilding of our sacred selves.

In this channeling St. Germaine reminds us not only of the tools at our fingertips, but most importantly the power of the Violet Flame.

"Greetings, I am St. Germaine. Welcome to this Council and to this time of healing as you prepare to jump forward on your chosen journey of life.

"The time of incubation, a time of standing back in observation, comes to an end. We speak to you now of healing not only of the Earth but of your own sacred self as you prepare to step forward into the wonder of who you are and into the wonder of Nova Earth. The time of inactivity is at an end.

"You are a race that Loves change and at the same time despises it. When it is not the change that you have asked for you disavow your participation. We always find it very humorous that you claim your place as co-creators and then back away when you deem that it is not in perfection.

"Dear heart, there is much debris that rises to the surface right now not only within your own sacred self, but within the community of mankind, womankind, animal-kind, all the elements, and all the creatures of all kingdoms. It comes forth for healing of everything that is not of wholeness prior to creation. It is not simply a matter of cleansing, for while there is much that is to simply be washed away there are other areas that need to be healed; corners of the soul, belief systems and places within your mind, pockets within your body. You say to me, beloved friend, 'How do I do this?' And so I tell you, it is as simple as igniting my Violet Flame within. With that essence of warmth and the power of cleansing, restoration and rejuvenation will take place.

"Many of you have forgotten the times when we have sat in Atlantis and healed the planet and humanity. It is important to use the tools at hand, which your Earth is being flooded with at this time. It is not a matter of redundancy; it is a matter of using these tools in concert for what one misses the other will get. It is not simply removal it is replenishment as well, so understand that.

"The usage of the Violet Flame as your primary tool will work wonders, it always has been because within the center of the flame is the I AM presence. It does not matter whether you are using the Violet Flame on your lungs or knees or heartbreak. It does not matter whether it is spiritual despair and isolation. It does not matter whether it is the soiling of the Earth and the planet. The Violet Flame will heal. I step forward this day to remind you that I have not disappeared. I am with you and I am very busy as you prepare to step forward, to heal yourself, heal your friends, your family, and your planet. Farewell."

St. Germaine continues on how each of us is changing the face of humanity.

"I have called each and every one of you forward, for there is need for transformers, healers, teachers, channels – they are all one in the same anyway. You are healers of the heart and this always entails the healing of the emotional and mental bodies. This includes the healing of Gaia, the healing of war and destruction. It is the healing not only of the distant wars but the war within.

"Our Mother, our beloved One, has asked all of us, above and below, to step forward during this time of dramatic change. Now let me be clear, I have no intention of assuming form again. And so my friends as I assist thee, it is you who effect these changes upon the planet. If you do not step forward, then who does? Who conducts the healing?

"There has been a time for integration. There has been a time even for silence. There has been a time to be the observer and to stand back. And now that time is over. It is time to move amongst the people and declare the joy, the simple joy of being in form. So when somebody asks you what you do, you can say, 'Oh, I am a Lightholder.' And they say, 'Well, what is that?' You can say, 'I'm a joy worker.' And they say, 'Well, what is that?' And you can say, 'I'm a pyromaniac. I go around lighting flames, building bonfires, and changing the face of humanity.'

"You are angels in form. You are the bravest of the brave. You are the showers of the way. Let us begin together and let it be graceful. Let it be gentle and sweet, for transformation has no need to be harsh. Yes, the energy is strong, but it is also wise. You, my friends, are deeply loved by so many above and below. If you receive nothing else from my heart, receive my Love, receive my honoring and the deep respect I have for each and every one of you. I am with you. I always have been. I always will be, for I AM. Farewell."

St. Germaine also speaks to us of our individual and collective mission as the creator race. We have journeyed through many phases of our physical and spiritual evolution. In terms of known human history we have continually evolved, moved out of the caves to hunter gathers to farmers to the industrial age to the electronic age to the information age – and now we are in the age of creation. We have evolved from being the primordial man to the creator race. This evolutionary jump is one of the most significant aspects of the Shift. It has positioned us so that we are prepared and equipped to enter into the full partnership of above and below in creating Nova Earth. This creation work is undertaken primarily from the fifth dimension and is part of the new abilities we are bringing forward.

"You are the creator race. That is how you are known throughout the intergalactic federation, as a race of master creators .You sit there shocked and awed – well, I was surprised when I first heard it too. You are creators. There are many myths on this planet and one of them was and is that you are created replica of Source and Creator. That is truth. You have demonstrated time and again your ability to create wonderful things, community and harmony, peace and prosperity, but you have also demonstrated your ability to create illusion and separation — belief systems that do not serve, death and destruction, war and hatred, but that part has been a dream, a part of your evolution. Now you are being called, each of you is being called, to step forward alone and to step forward together to create your new world, and, it is a world based on Love, on the ability to exist in form, and to be sheer energy in form. Seldom has this happened in other Universes and galaxies. What has occurred in other galaxies when the energy or species has evolved to collective unity of One, when the mind and heart has become One and the energy has become unified as Love, is that form or physicality was released.

"The creator race is going to create a new form, Nova Being, a physical form that is the sheer energy of Love. That is your job, your mission. That is your choice, your purpose, your service and that is the only reason you are healers. It is to expand yourself and everybody on this planet to this place of unification where the uniqueness of the form is absolutely reveled in, in joy to the fullest, and released at will. This planet is a reflection of the diversity of the mind and the will of One. That is why you all look different. It is that wonderful freedom of choice.

"You are doing this job and I will attend to you and I will guide you and remind you that you are whole, that you are loved and that all is possible, that the illusion of limitation is but a dream. You may live in your form for a thousand years or you may leave it in an instant, the choice is yours. And you have already chosen to stay."

In a subsequent channeling St. Germaine continues his explanation of the creator race and our role within that collective.

"I am St. Germaine, and I come this day to speak to you of creativity, of creation, and of the energy that you carry within yourself that has been gifted to you, not only from me, but from every master and every saint and from the Godhead. It is the gift of creation.

"The Mother has not birthed an inferior race. She has birthed children of her heart and children of her essence, and that is why you are creators. It has been imbedded within you and the most basic function of all, the ability to reproduce, to procreate; it is a profound reminder of your role as creator race. My brothers and sisters of Earth and far beyond, it is time for us to create yet again.

"Long ago we sat in my temple, the Temple of the Violet Flame in Atlantis, in the most beautiful paradise on Earth. We have reveled and we have celebrated and we have healed many and enjoyed physicality. When we saw the chaos rise, we decided to allow many to exercise their free will, to follow their path, believing that they would find their way home to their hearts. We did not interfere with their choices and decisions, nor would I suggest that you do so now. But what we did not do, my brothers and sisters, was to create an equal force, a force of creation of Love, of compassion and healing that would override and show the light to those who had lost their way. We believed in our hearts, in the honoring of the path of others, and we trusted in the unfoldment of the Universe. So we watched as our beloved continent was destroyed; from arrogance yes, but also from our own lack of action, from our own inertia, from our own unwillingness to accept our role as co-creators upon this planet.

"That is why we re-established this Temple of the Violet Flame today. That is why I guide you. We have told you of the rerun, of the repeat of the scenario of Atlantis at this time, but we will take action this time. Together, hand in hand, in healing heart, we will create Nova Earth, the place where none is left in desolation of darkness believing they are unloved. We will care enough to shine the brightest light into the darkest places, to go to the places of chaos, to endure with fortitude, and we will do so because we know we have the support not only of each other, but of all our friends and allies above and below.

"Your numbers on Earth are legion of those who believe in the creation of Love, of peace, of a different way of existence. And those who say they do not simply do so because they feel powerless and they do not know any other way to proceed. So instill my Violet Flame this day within everybody's heart, every person, dog, cat, alligator, bird, tree, fish and farm and let it burn brightly. Let this flame incinerate the old ways so that never again will we sit and watch the destruction of what we Love. It is not a matter, my friends, of generator crystals or bombs, it is the destruction of the human spirit that is in danger and that is what you heal. That is the essence of creation that you have been given directly from the heart of the Mother and Father God.

"I have asked you many times to dream, for it is not enough to sit in reverence and say, 'I will heal the planet.' Dream of your new tomorrow, of what you choose to create in your every waking moment, from the moment you get out of bed to the moment you go to sleep. Dream your daily reality and dream your Earth. Dream your place at this Intergalactic Council for they await you. It is time for you to move freely, not only over Earth but amongst the stars. We have traveled in many places, healing many Universes, and now we return to Earth together to create from our very essence the promise of long ago. You have glimpsed it. You have glimpsed it in your inner eye. You are created in wholeness and I will help you remember that. I will pick up my shovel and my pick and I will chip away at resistance, and I will dig you a foxhole so you will feel protected and move forward, but not alone.

"Move forward in laughter and joy. Creation does not take place in sorrow and pain. It jumps out of the silence in joyous recognition of possibility. It leaps into action from the place of nothingness. You know this. Each one of you knows this. So when you heal each other, when you conduct your meditation of peace on Sunday night, instill the Violet Flame into absolutely everything you can think of and then go to the place of stillness. Dream your dream and then Monday morning leap into action. I will be there to catch you. Go in peace. Farewell."

Although this next St. Germaine channeling speaks of healing Gaia as we prepare for the arrival of our star brothers and sisters, I also believe it speaks very clearly to our role as gatekeepers. Again gatekeepers are those who will or have ascended to the fifth through seventh dimensions and who reach back to help our human brothers and sisters through the Ascension portal.

"It is important that you continue to send healing to Gaia, this mighty being. Do not dismiss her or overlook her needs because you believe she is mighty and strong.

"If you had a dear heart-friend who was going through tumultuous changes, no matter how strong or how consistent or how anchored you believed they are, still you would stand by them. And you would extend your hands and your heart and you would say 'What can I do to help? I know you are strong and self-sufficient, and I know you are whole.' But during times of upheaval, the human examples death, divorce, loss of Love, illness, setbacks, finances, when you saw someone hit with all of these you would say 'Let me help you steady up.' And if it was only simply to sit with them and to put your hands on their heart or to send healing, you would do so. And you would certainly ask me to reinforce them so that they could go forward in their journey. And so it is with Gaia.

"One of the things that Gaia is doing is preparing herself for the reception of new energies, certainly new inter-dimensional energies, for this one is much further along in her progress in Ascension than humanity. But she is also preparing to receive visitors, your star brothers and sisters. And it is just like if you were having company, if I was coming to dinner, you would clean the house. That is what is going on.

"The Council of Love has said many times that peace must reign on Earth in order for the Ascended Masters to walk, but also for your star brothers and sisters to walk. The stage is already set; many heads of state are already in agreement. What we are asking is not only for the elimination of fear but the insertion of peaceful welcome, of openheartedness; of the recognition of the I AM Presence in all beings and all things. This is the healing of the Violet Flame that I wish you to focus upon right now, tomorrow, and the day after, and until this mission is completed. To see in each person's heart, whether it is a five-year old or a ninety-year old, whether it is an African, an American, an Innu, a European, it matters not. See the entire planet open-armed, welcoming in a spirit of peace and Love which means a healing of fear and trepidation of the different.

"You can do this and you can help. The human collective has need for the arrival of their star brothers and sisters. They may not know it but they will benefit greatly from the gifts of science, of technology, of the exchange of cultures, of the fulfillment of the Cities of Light. So I ask for your help, and more importantly, I thank you for it because I already know your heart."

Before we move on to the initiation into the Violet Flame of St. Germaine I wish to share with you a clearing meditation with this Master that works miracles. This has been given to us specifically as part of the Ascension process and preparation, an exercise that helps us heal third dimensional paradigms within ourselves, mostly based on lack and limitation, in order that we can be pure vessels of Light and Love in service to humanity.

We all experience times when we either do or don't feel aligned with our higher self and, regardless, situations, issues or illness will arise and we question why. We feel there is no way our soul or higher self would have chosen this particular burden.

So, let's be really practical and do a little meditation about some aspect of either our body or our life that you are unhappy with, because I'll lay odds that what you are identifying is part of the old grid of the third dimension. In fact, I know it. Remember, you have read earlier about the old paradigms of death, disease, destruction, lack, limitation, greed, control, lust, and all those other nasties. Often we tend to think of limitation in terms of physicality. We think how little we have or how little we can pay for something, but limitation can also mean limitation of air flow, limitation of chi. And we know throughout God force, throughout the Universe, there's no limitation of life force energy and yet there's days when we feel like we are down and sometimes it's because it's time to lay down and just relax; but sometimes it's because we're caught in that false grid of limitation.

Meditation – Removal of Old Grids

Take a nice deep breath and really relax. Relax and breathe, take a nice deep breath of purple and it's that beautiful purple of our beloved St. Germaine. It's that purple of chrysanthemums and woodland violets and pansies. It's the liturgical purple and purple popsicles and Welch's Grape Juice; breathe in and smell the purple, the grape and bring it down into your heart.

We ask St. Germaine, our beloved master of Violet Flame to help us with this healing, with this removal exercise, with this mini-psychic surgery.

Go into your heart and rest there and let go of the day, and let go of the week, and just be. As you sit feel yourself becoming heavier and heavier, you couldn't move off your chair if you tried. Know that you are in a place of calm, serenity, and that you're safe.

Think of one thing, just one thing, you are currently experiencing in your life you do not feel you want to continue experiencing or that is not in keeping with your higher self, and the unfoldment of your plan. Just one thing. Go deeper into your heart and be honest with yourself, because we are going to peel the onion here. Feel it. Often when we have these feelings they come forward as lack. It can be lack of a relationship, lack of self-esteem or self-Love; lack of good health; of that feeling of being vibrant; of being in perfect alignment with your body; lack of a good relationships with our family; or lack of money.

Feel that essence of what it is that you want to let go of in your life, you just have darn well had enough of. Stay in your heart but you may feel it elsewhere in your body, in your gut, your sacral, your root, your chest, your solar plexus, your back, your shoulders, even in your head and your face, but you're going to feel it somewhere in your body.

And breathe.

Now, staying in your heart, isolate that spot on your body where this situation or lack is located. For example, if you're feeling it in your solar plexus isolate it so that you can feel it as a ball or clump in one particular spot rather than your entire solar plexus. Take a moment to really pinpoint it, and, when you do I want you to take one or both of your hands and touch that spot on your body, and, Love that energy that has frustrated you so much.

Love it, give it compassion. Compassion does not assume the energy, it simply understands the situation. Let the Love and the Violet Flame flow through your hands into this place on your body. Now leave your hand there, come back into your heart.

And breathe.

Now, bring yourself up into the Thirteenth Octave. Go up that golden spiral to the heart of One. Feel that alignment.

And breathe.

Mother and Father are laying you on a table, it looks like an altar, its crystal and beautiful and it shimmers with the light and you can feel the presence not only of the mighty archangels but the circle of the pink angels surrounding you.

"I AM St. Germaine, Master and Keeper of the Violet Flame,

Keeper of the I AM Presence, Keeper of thee my beloved friends. You do not need to carry what does not serve you; you do not need to carry it for a greater cause. There have been many times in the past where you have processed and carried for the collective, but it is time for you to be pure vessels of Light and pure vessels of Love, and that is the work of healing and transmission that you do. You are my new armada and you radiate this energy out to all beings throughout the galaxies.

"This magnificent energy is amplified as it leaves your portal and travels outward at the speed of Love. It travels everywhere including your planet. You do not need to carry the burdens that you have carried willingly and unknowingly in the past. When Archangel Gabrielle has said the rules of engagement have changed, she has meant it. And so this is part of how things have and are shifting. So I come this day humbly as physician and friend to relieve you of this burden, to relieve you of this situation that is not of Nova Earth, not of Love, not of the Cities of Light, not of the higher dimensions.

"First I ask your sacred permission, I ask for your vow to let go, for never will I or any of us intrude on your free will, for that is not of Love. You say 'yes' to me and I accept this for I see the look in your eyes, I see not only the permission but the plea for relief. So lay comfortably my friend. Remove your hand from the place of sorrow and let me use my light saber, my torch to remove this burden from you once and for all.

"I do not do this for the whole of humanity; I do it for you because of our Love and our enduring relationship. Be still sweet one for a moment while we do this. Now, I reseal you and I fill this gap with Blue Diamond of the Mother and my thread is the violet thread; it is the thread of life, it is the weaving of One. I know you have been given many, many gifts for elimination but when you have need of me, come to this sacred place of Mother/Father/One and call me. I will be with you to help. Now rest, I will watch over you, we all will.

"Enough with clearing, I invite you now to join me in the Temple of the Violet Flame. I have waited for you and for this reunion for thousands of years, so I will await while you prepare yourself and make yourself comfortable. I Love you, my beloved friend."

Now that you have cleared away your old belief systems you are ready to proceed to the initiation into the Temple of the Violet Flame. But allow yourself some time to integrate what has just taken place. Remember this is a process not a race.

A word of advice before you start the meditation. The initiation is about half an hour but you may be floating for hours so make sure you are comfortable, have some water close by – and probably some Kleenex. And if you have a candle, white or purple, light it beforehand. And enjoy.

• Listen to "Temple of the Violet Flame" audio file to undergo the initiation into St. Germaine's Temple of the Violet Flame.

Congratulations, and welcome into the Temple of the Violet Flame. The Violet Flame is that all-purpose tool that you can call on again and again. This is part of you for the rest of your life – and beyond. The flames of transmutation, of the I AM Presence, are burning brightly in your palms, fingertips, heart, third eye and crown chakras. You may use the Violet Flame as a single small flame or as a blazing bonfire. Discernment and practice are the key. But know you can't go wrong.

Enjoy this gift and sensation. And then when you are ready proceed to the next chapter on the gift of Universal Mother Mary's Blue Diamond. It's better than any birthday – the gifts just keep coming.

Naturally before you proceed to the Blue Diamond, St Germaine has some further understandings he wants to share.

"My beloved friends, each of you carry the element of fire, albeit some more obvious than others. There are numerous references in your languages to this innate understanding; fire in the belly, flames in your heart; your mind on fire with inspiration and ideas; kundalini flames climbing up your spine; and on fire with desire. What we have done in this initiation is ignite those fires to a higher level. We have turned up the heavenly gas. We have tinged those fires with a beautiful shade of violet, with the Divine Gift of the I AM Presence. We have focused that fire energy to be used by and for you in this wondrous journey of Ascension. But it is also the gift of healing, so my beloveds, I beseech you to share it magnanimously, humbly and with laughter. Be on fire with the desire to transform your world and collective. Now I turn you over to our blessed Divine Mother for the gift of her essence. Go in peace."

Chapter 5

Universal Mother Mary's Gift
of the Blue Diamond

It was one of those perfect sunny, lazy days I was spending with friends during the time I lived in Sedona, Ariz., in 2002. We went hiking by Cathedral Rock, one of the energy vortexes in Sedona that represents balance and harmony of the male and female energies. We stopped by Oak Creek to rest and do a little meditation, the energy between us all was sweet and strong.

I can't tell you to this day that as I lay there on the warm rocks listening to the babble of the creek and the blessed silence whether my eyes were open or closed, but all of the sudden when I looked up at the sky it was raining Blue Diamonds. It was as if someone had peeled back the sky like a huge piece of cellophane and there was a shower of incredible Blue Diamonds floating down to Earth covering everything, including my friends and me. The air was alive with sparkles of blue. It felt like it was snowing Blue Diamonds and we should just stick our tongues out like kids in the first snowstorm of winter.

If you have ever been in the fallout of a major fire or volcano, you know how the ash simply floats in the air and covers the Earth and everything on her. This was leagues prettier than any ash I had ever seen, and it was everywhere! It wasn't stopping and there was an amazing sweetness in the air. The scent of roses was pervasive. As the Blue Diamonds landed on my skin I could feel a tingling sensation and then it sunk in. It didn't dissolve, it sank in. Bit of a shocker, but boy did it feel heavenly. Of course we immediately had to know what on Earth, and in heaven, was going on. But before I could even begin to channel or ask, Universal Mother Mary came in and began telling us about her gift of her essence, the gift of the Blue Diamond energy. The rest, as they say, is history.

Think about it, let this sink into your consciousness and your heart. The Blue Diamond energy is the very essence of the Divine Mother. We have a saying dust to dust, here on Earth. When someone dies or releases their form all that is left of them, all you can see is their essence, or their dust. If you are of the emerald ray, for example, then when you dissolve what we are left with is that wonderful dust or sparkling energies of emerald. And each person is unique in the essence of their energies or dust. It is part of the gift of each of us.

The essence, the soul matter of the Universal Mother is the most incredible dazzling Blue Diamond energy imaginable. It is the most brilliant clear diamond united with the perfect blue sapphire. Incredible is too mild a word – amazing, extraordinary, fantastic – nothing comes close to fully describing this dust. It is the core of the Universal Mother and she has freely given it to us as a gift from her heart to the whole of humanity; which is overwhelming. And what did we do to deserve it? More aptly how could we ever do anything spectacular enough to deserve it? Nothing. It is simply a gift, a blessing from her heart to ours.

This is the gift of Universal Mother Mary's very essence, originally gifted in 2002 and has been continually renewed ever since that momentous day. The Blue Diamond is not something from our beloved Mother, it is Her – Her Love, Her nurturing, Her healing transmitted directly into your heart and core. It is our anchoring of the Divine Feminine within our beings, including our physical bodies.

Our sacred Divine Mother explains it this way: "I give you my essence, my very core of Blue Diamond so that you would be filled with Mother's Love but also with my power, with my nurturing, with my knowledge, with my wisdom, with my strength, with my endurance, and, my patience. All of this is part and parcel now not only of who I am but of who you are. This blessing is not a selective gift. Each of you on Earth are continually infused with my essence of Blue Diamond. And I will do this until you return home and far after if you wish."

For purposes of this Ascension process, Universal Mother Mary repeats her promise: "I give you my essence of Blue Diamond yet again, so you will know that I am within you, around you, next to you, above, below and in every cranny and crevice in between. We are not separate. The gift of the nova grid of humanity is unity; unity, community, and connectedness. It is the joy of knowing you are unique in any universe and you are exactly the same. It's the beauty of creation. I invite you, my sacred souls, children of my heart, to join with me to go through this Ascension portal of Oneness and beyond. It is time for your next step."

It's funny how we all think we comprehend a blessing or situation. Initially when the gift of the Blue Diamond was bestowed upon us I felt for sure "this is it – here we go, we're ready for Ascension; we're all ready for the Shift – we've got what we need." I mean how could it get any better than receiving the essence of the Mother?

Of course as time goes on we come to more fully understand the nature of the gift – that it was for the healing of humanity, of our hearts, the deepening and perhaps really the concrete beginning of our new partnership matrix with the Divine realms. We needed that Divine Mother essence to nurture us back to wholeness and help us begin to believe in ourselves as co-creators of Nova Earth. It has only been in the past couple of years with the further gifts of the Pink Diamond and Yahweh's Golden Flame that the full import is being more fully understood. The Blue Diamond is part of our Tri-Flame, the ignition of which is necessary for Ascension. It was and is the Blue Diamond that ignites our Tri-Flame.

And yet, I feel we don't have the full story yet. The one thing I have come to realize in working with the Council is there is always more; the infinite nature of the Universe always has something more, something greater, up their eternal sleeves.

The essence of the Blue Diamond is used extensively in healing and creation work. The instilling of this energy into a person or a situation has remarkable results in restoring balance and wholeness – whether it is to a broken leg, a broken marriage or restoring world peace. How the gift of the Blue Diamond is activated is through intent and visualization. Visualize instilling that sparkling blue into the depleted area of whichever body (physical, mental emotional, causal, spiritual) calls out for it. It can also be accomplished by placing your hands in the diamond position and placing it over the area of need either in person or remotely. It can be very powerful by simply opening your heart and requesting the Mother to fill you. She will, always, and the shift it creates within is beyond any form of healing we know.

Even though it has been ten years since this miraculous intervention was bestowed upon Earth and humanity, we are still learning about the fullness of its potential. I refer to the work that we will do not only in the Ascension process but with our brothers and sisters of the stars, and the anchoring of the Cities of Light. Mother Mary has hinted at some of those connections:

"I give you this gift of my Blue Diamond. It is my gentle radiance with the power to fuel many Universes. It will give you the strength to continue onward. It will give you the fuel to propel you forward into new realities. I welcome you this day as Nova Beings to Nova Earth. You are reborn, a small innocent baby. Rejoice in this and enter naked, without the baggage of your old self into this wondrous place of new Earth, true Earth, to my garden of pure joy. I invite you, each one of you to enter through the portal of your heart into and through this portal of my heart.

"I wish for you to experience this planet and this Universe as I have created it and there is nothing dense or solid about it. Yes, you may experience the collection of energy as solid matter and form, but do not delude yourself child. Begin anew this day in the new reality that you and I have co-created.

"Do you wonder, my children, about the inhabitants of the Cities of Light? Who lives in these cities? Yes, your inter-dimensional brothers and sisters join you there, but you my brilliant beacons, my bringers and holders of Light; you are also the inhabitants of these cities. These are not abandoned, vacant cities. They are vibrant, filled with sound and color, music and joy, with creativity, art and beauty. They are to be places of healing, creativity, contentment and laughter if you simply acknowledge my plan. You have been working; all of you, on these cities for a very long time without knowing it. How you have been doing this is by working and accepting your sacred self.

"But the time for work is over child. Now, it is time for play. Earth and the Cities of Light are not places of drudgery or greed. That is why so many cities are currently being cleansed, that the new, which is the ancient, may emerge. It is part of my gift and it is part of your gift to the planet and to each other, to allow yourselves to raise yourselves up, to be the multi-dimensional beings that you have always been in form on this new planet of Love, on this ancient planet that I have birthed.

"Understand, dear heart, that my Blue Diamond is also part of the halion ray, the essence of many of your brothers and sisters of the stars. You carry this halion within your DNA and essence. To this halion, I have added my Blue Diamond particularly to the human race. I remind you of the importance of that combination of the halion and Blue Diamond gifts. This combination gives you the ability to create and to go forward as Nova Beings who have the key to whichever galaxy, whichever reality, whichever dimension you choose. It is yours to choose."

The Universal Mother has also requested that we include the gifts of her Clear Blue energy which was bestowed upon us in 2003, and her Blue Flame, which was given in 2009. Mother Mary is quite insistent that it is the combination of the three blue elements that are and will assist us in our Ascension process. The Mother's Clear Blue Light appears as soft blue and transparent, a great deal like a clear blue crystal. It is used in the much the same way as the Blue Diamond, invoked by intent and received through allowance, particularly through the heart chakra.

Mother Mary's Clear Blue Light & The Creator Race

"Greetings I am Mary, Universal Mother and Mother of Creation. Welcome my beloved children, children of my heart and of my soul. We do not interfere in the affairs of humanity, and we allow always the exercise of free will. However, I do interject at this point as I bathe my daughter, my planet Terra Nova, and each one of you in my light of Clear Blue. There is clear alignment of the planets, of the energies throughout many Universes and it is time for you to embrace yourself, individually and collectively, fully and wholly as the creator race.

"There is much fear upon the planet of what you will choose to create, for you have witnessed time and time again, the creation of abomination. But dear ones this is not the reality of your heart, it is not the reality of your soul, and it is not what my children will bring forth on Terra Nova. It is time to embrace your power for what is created as new upon this Earth is the creation of humankind, of each one of you.

"The angels and Archangels, the Legions of Light, the Unified Forces of the Outer Galaxies (UFOG) will not descend upon the planet during this initial period of reconstruction; they will not be the ones to repair the Gaia and to create the garden. You are the legions of light, you are the dear ones that have said to me 'Mother, I will go forward and I will clear the Earth, and I will teach and live and be Love.'

"This planet of my birthing was created solely as a place of beauty, for that is why spirit would assume form, to dance amongst the rocks and trees, the deserts and oceans. It was intended to be an oasis, so beautiful that spirits from far and wide would say 'let us go, let us visit this place of diversity, of such beauty that it invites and entices the expression of Love.' Much has happened with the evolution of free will, much of the surface of the planet has been sullied; it matters not for all is forgiven. Gaia herself has compassion for those who would rape and mutilate.

"The human race, the creator race, has grown up; they leave the old ways of destruction, of separation behind. Each one of you, look in the mirror and see you are my children. I do not speak in metaphors – you are of my womb, of my essence, and the splendid design that you have created in concert with One long ago. It is time for that essence and design, to create in form. It is not enough, my children, for humanity to simply live in peace, meaning the absence of war, for true peace comes from the creation of deeper beauty, the sharing of One.

"This creation of beauty is not simply to be done by a few individuals but by each and every person who has assumed form and walks this planet. From time to time there have been those who have come among you to teach how to create. However, it is no longer sufficient to have a master or two in form, it is required and time for each one of you to step forward and create what your heart desires, for we trust your heart. It is not gridded in selfishness and lust, it is a flower blossoming in springtime. It is a joy to all who behold it above and below.

"Step out of fear, out of limitation my children and begin to create each day that which you desire. Please, we ask of you to make this concrete so that you will come to understand that we are not speaking of esoteric practice but of the reality of human existence.

"Many of you already understand this – you are the gardeners of the planet. You plant the seeds and you watch the flowers grow. Personal creation is no different; you plant the seed into your heart, you drop it into the still point, you water it and protect it, allow the sun to draw it out from the deepest part of you and to flower upon the Earth. While you are doing this you do not simply sit and stare at the place in the dirt where you have planted the seed. You go forward, you create an entire garden, and you go about your life. That is what I am asking of each of you.

"Make your life, every thought, every action, every breath a creation of beauty, an expression of your vision of beauty upon the planet. Make this a daily practice and allow it to come forward. Do not be the gardener who goes and uproots the seed or the tender sprout because of anxiety or because you think you have failed because it has not come forward. Leave it be and let it come in divine timing. There is a season of planting and creation, and it is that season upon the Earth. It is the cycle of life. You have the sun and you have my light of clear blue that is penetrating all, and which will clear doubt and fear and calm the heart. Do this daily my children; allow your garden to grow. Go with my Love and my blessings. Farewell."

The use and purpose of the Universal Mother's gift of her Clear Blue Light is, as she says, to clear doubt and fear, disillusion, and to plant clarity and serenity within your being.

One of the areas Lightworkers experience the greatest challenge is in manifesting – in bringing into form what you are working on, be it financial abundance, love relationships, healing or resolving a difficult situation. In this following channeling Mother Mary explains how her Blue Flame of Hope works to move us from hope and trust into stillness, action and manifestation. She reminds us that she always responds to our prayers and invites us to join in creation partnership with her. Count me in!

Mother Mary's Blue Flame of Hope and Co-Creation

"Greetings I am Mary, welcome children of my heart, my legion of light, my peaceful warriors. Come to me as I come to you, not as distant matriarch but as mother who loves you; who tends to you. I want to be clear – it is not that I wish to tend to you; I simply do tend to you, to each and every one of you. The more you allow me to tend to you the happier I am and the more I will do. Sweet angels, I have asked the channel to remind you of my cloak of blue that I so gladly give and share with you – but I also wish to remind you this day of my Blue Flame of hope.

"Hope is what is required in the bleakest moments when you feel that you are being overcome by confusion, despair or abandonment. When you are looking around and you can't see what you are looking for, you are seeking your sweet self, your true self. It is much easier to hope, and to hold hope and trust when things are smooth, when they are going well. However, it is also essential to do so when life appears to be in turmoil because then you build on the hope. When you have the hope and trust it moves into stillness and action and manifestation.

"Do not forget that the beginning of manifestation, of creation, even prior to intent is having my Blue Flame of hope in your heart. If you do not have the hope and the trust, then the formulation of intent is futile; you are wasting your time. I have imbedded my blue flame of hope in each one of your hearts. You can hope for small things or you can hope for large things – I do not sit here and sort by category. When that plea of hope and that belief of trust is directed to me I always respond. If you feel that I do not respond in the way that you anticipate or expect or want, then I ask you to trust me that there is an unfoldment that is better – and it is not just for my unfoldment but for yours – for my plan is inclusive of yours.

"Do not turn away from me. I have said to you that I will show up in every living room if that is what it takes for you to trust me and come to know me. I sit with you to co-create, to weave your dreams into reality that expresses in your third dimension. For this is where Nova Earth is located. Yes, you will ascend into the seventh (dimension) – you are already there in so many ways, but you manifest in the third .

"It is important above and below that you fully understand that this is a time of manifestation, and at this moment manifestation is from the seventh or the fifth into the third dimension.

"When I have asked all of you to step forward it is not just to stand there. Stepping forward is manifestation, it is creating, it is bringing forth whether it is a change in attitude, which is an expression of the heart, whether it is the healing of the planet, or the healing of a particular community. This is manifestation of holding hope, stepping forward and taking action. It is a continuum my children, it is a process. It is not distinct steps that feel individuated – i.e., now I am holding intention, now I am at still point, now I am in action – it is a flow. Think of creation as the infinity sign flowing back and forth cocooned by gratitude and Love. It is a basic Universal Law; this is how things work on your planet.

"I want to teach you, I want to show you, I want to create in partnership with you. I want to sit and rejoice when you manifest what your heart desires. And then I want to plan with you again as you start again. As a mother, when your baby starts to crawl you do not turn away and say "that is beautiful – my job is done". No, you watch as they begin to walk, and then run, and then venture forth into the world.

"I am your Mother for eternity, turn to me in that way, share your fears and give them to me, share your dreams and show me how they manifest – if you need my help I am here. I will never let you down. I am so proud of you and I Love you – each and every one of you. I Love you with my whole heart. Go in peace. Farewell."

So often Universal Mother Mary has said to us "if there is no hope, there is no life; if there is no trust, there is no Love." So heed these messages and incredible offers of assistance directly from the heart of the Divine Mother. Take advantage of your birthright and begin. Take a minute and do the following meditation with the Blue Diamond Energy of the Divine Feminine.

Meditation

Begin by taking a nice deep breath of absolutely clear energy. No color. Just that beautiful crystal clear, and breathe it in and sink down to your heart and relax and let go of the day, of the week, of all of you responsibilities, everything that needs to be done and just be. Just take this time for yourself, of your connection with the Council of Love. Relax and allow let this energy flood you.

Pause and breathe.

In your left hand, with your palm up, I want you to see the most beautiful, clear, white diamond of intense purity, glorious brilliance. Its perfection is stunning and the facets shine. You can feel the energy not only in your hand, but emanating from your hand into your heart. It is generating rainbows all around the room.

Pause and breathe.

Now in your right hand feel yourself with a beautiful blue, dark blue sapphire. This comes from the depth of the Earth, but it has been restored and it is brilliant and it been displayed in the halls of Atlantis as an object of art and beauty. Hold that in your hand as well. Feel the coolness of the Atlantic Ocean and the brilliance of the Pleiades and then blend of elements that have created this beautiful sapphire. Feel that energy as it penetrates into your being and you feel the blue in your heart and throat, third eye, and open.

Pause and breathe.

Now take your hands and bring these two stones together. Bring your hands together with the beautiful, white, crystal diamond and the beautiful, blue sapphire. Cup your hands together and merge these two beautiful stones and all the elements that lie within. Now open your hands and see this radiant third diamond with luster, shine and brilliance beyond anything you have ever witnessed. The power, the energy that is emanating from it almost feels too hot, too big, too mighty to hold.

Pause and breathe.

Now, take this Blue Diamond and bring it up to your heart with both your hands and place it in your heart, directly into the center. Let it in. Feel it. The pulsating beams enter into your very core as it travels in your nervous system, your endocrine system, your circulation, your blood. Feel the rays as the emanate out from you, out the back of you, out of the front of you, out your crown and down to the Earth for a stone of this brilliance cannot be hidden. Anchor it firmly in your heart that you may call on this energy at any moment, in any situation. And know that as you walk the world you radiate the sacred essence of the Mother, her Blue Diamond.

Then when you are ready simply come back, anchor firmly in the heart of Gaia and go about your day.

Years ago, when I first began teaching about the rays and chakras and the power of colors, people would often get nervous and say what if I'm not clear; what if I don't see any color; basically what if I make a mistake. Archangel Gabrielle gave some very wise advice at that time that still holds true today: "When in doubt think white." That is absolutely true, you can never go wrong by bringing in that beautiful bright shining white light.

However, seeing we are concluding this section on the various gifts of Mary's blue I would also like to say you can never go wrong with blue either; the blues of the Universal Mother, the blue of Archangel Michael, the blue of Gaia, of Electra and so forth. Blue is the color of change, it is the ray of hope, it is the ray of communication and the ray of the spiritual warrior. During this time of Shift, of Ascension into a new realm of existence, never hesitate to use blue – it will never let you down.

Earlier in this chapter I spoke of a knowing that the use of the Mother's Blue Diamond is still growing and unfolding. We have not reached completion of this magnificent gift as yet. In closing I would like to share with you a message I channeled on February 18, 2012 from the Mother our next assignment with the Blue Diamond.

"Greetings, I AM Mary, Universal Mother, Mother of Hope, Mother of Change, Mother of Love. Welcome, welcome my beloved angels, hybrids, star seeds, all beings of Light and Love. Welcome to this Council and to this circle of One. Welcome home.

"I ask you to keep your Tri-Flame burning brightly and to attach firmly and completely to the heart of Gaia. But sweet angels there is more; there is a massive wave of healing and restoration that is underway and I ask each of you within your hearts for your assistance.

"It is part of going forward, whether you call it Ascension, Shift, or simply remaining in Love, it matters not. Many of your brothers and sisters of Earth are suffering; they are suffering alone and in the dark. And yes, they can be surrounded by a million people and they are still suffering alone and in the dark. What I ask of you, as a circle, as a collective, as an individual, every day, to see that you are sending this Blue Diamond of my essence, adding your efforts to mine, for we are in divine partnership; and sending it to every bereft soul upon the planet. And you say to me 'well Mother, how do I know who is bereft and who isn't?' Well you don't. And it does not matter because you can never receive too much Blue Diamond; you can never have an overdose of my essence and my Love. No matter how many times I say this to you as I look at you, as I look at your hearts, you still do not fully comprehend what I am saying and offering to you.

"I am the Universal Mother. I have birthed, not only each of you, but many universes. I am in trinity with All. I am Light, I am energy, I am far beyond what you think of as form. Many of you think of me in my form as Mary, mother of Jesus, and that is a form I cherish, or the Virgin of Fatima, of Guadalupe, it matters not. I wish you for a moment to simply feel the totality of my being. Pause, breathe and allow.

"In the way that each of you, right now, have skin and bones, hair and eyes, blood and sweat, dreams and fervor, the ability to create and to destroy, you are a mirror of the Divine Masculine and I. You always have been. But if you think or feel my skin and bones, my dreams and creation, it is simply like a Milky Way, far bigger, of Blue Diamond: beyond imagination.

"I am always and infinitely, eternally creating; there is always more. And I wish to share this with you, children of my heart. All of us have been beckoning you home, up that golden spiral, up, yes to the Thirteenth Octave, but not out of body, carrying it, raising it. Let us help and let us help humanity receive my gift.

"If you must, think of it as your service, your responsibility, that word you avoid, to receive my gift of Blue Diamond. Let me flood you in this moment; let me fill you with my nurturing and my Love. Do not limit this, do not turn away. And when I ask you to transmit this to the collective, see that you are not sending it just from your own being, but with me you are standing well above the planet. You are peeling back the sky for me, with me, and you are allowing this beautiful shower of Blue Diamond to fill every human being upon the planet; the poor, the disenfranchised, the hungry, the rich, the wealthy, those who believe themselves to be powerful. There is no being that does not require it, especially at this time.

"This is what I ask of thee and this is what I offer you, not just my Love, but my being, my essence. Take it, cherish it, but do not hoard it, there is always more. Let it flow freely and clearly throughout all of your being. As you grow and expand, the

Blue Diamond is essential in your creation work. Use it; sprinkle it in your intent and your actions. It will bring things to fruition much more quickly; it is like a pinch of salt to the stew.

We are here, never to control but always, always to help, to love. I AM your Mother. Go in peace. Farewell.

Chapter 6

Gift of the Pink Diamond

The gift of the Pink Diamond energy sneaked up on us. For months, I kept seeing pink diamonds wherever I looked and simply thought that it was Mother Mary showing us how multi-faceted her energy is and the different ways that it can manifest. Then as I prepared for the 2009 Annual COL Gathering, the theme of which was Love, she began to talk about the gift of her Pink Diamond, distinct and very different than the Blue Diamond energy. The gift of the Pink Diamond is for the anchoring of the totality of your divinity within your core, within your physical and expanded selves. With the healing of the Blue Diamond we have reached a point where we are ready to accept and anchor the glory of our own sweet beings.

After years anchoring the Blue Diamond of healing, nurturing and co-creation of Nova Earth, our beloved Divine Mother stepped forward to gift us with the Pink Diamond. This energy is the activation and anchoring of our wholeness – of all of our aspects, a renewed grid, our soul design, and most importantly a deep unconditional connection, acceptance, acknowledgement and Love of who we are, here and now on Earth, in form. You cannot Love fully or completely or be genuinely part of community, if you are not in a place of love for your sacred self.

It is with incredible joy that I share the Pink Diamond attunement with each of you. Open your heart, relax and receive.

"Greetings, I am Mary, Universal Mother and I welcome each and every one of you, my angels of pink. You travel upon a myriad of rays, many of you preferring blue, as do I. And yet who do we surround ourselves with? Who are those who sit, create and play but the angels of pink? For they are the ones who have remained close to home, and they are the ones who are the most beautiful. They are not only beautiful because of their physicality, of what you would think of anyway as physicality, they are beautiful because of who they are.

"Why have these angels of pink who guard the throne of One remained with us? Because we are united in heart. We are united in purpose. We are united in the creation of the multiverse. It is from this place of heart connection, of Love, of being forever in the state of grace that this retinue of angels surrounds us. And, dear heart, they also surround you in this very moment, which is highly unusual for they do not leave the doorway of Heaven. But I have asked of them to surround you and encircle you for this time together as you move with me to a place beyond dimension, retaining your physicality.

"Each of you, as you incarnated, have turned to me and said 'Mother, I will go, for I believe in your plan.' It is the unfoldment of the plan of Love on the planet of Love. Although there has been much density and what we would call disillusion you have come to this planet in service to me. It has not always been easy to be in that flux of change as energies are shifting rapidly and dramatically, as frequencies are being raised and the old is being eliminated. We are fully aware of what you experience. We are not on some distant cloud, child. We are with you. We are with you in every way that you can possibly conceive of.

"Often we have conversations, and I say to you, 'I love you. I love you as my child, as my friend, as my angel in form, as my pathfinder, as my sister and brother.' However, I do not feel that you have fully understood and known in the deepest part of you consistently; moment after moment, day after day the truth of that Love. No, I do not criticize. I simply want you to know the extent, the breath, the truth and depth of my Love. It is everexpanding. It is not limited. I did not say I will give you a cup of my Blue Diamond and there you go. It is an eternal wellspring that you are free to draw upon, and I invite you to do so. I want all this to be clear before we speak of the Pink Diamond because I want you to think of the Blue Diamond as my Love and everything that that entails.

"Sometimes you say to me 'Oh, I have prayed, I have done my creation exercise, and I have not received.' Dear ones, there is such a thing as divine timing. And as most of you know, divine timing is also Mother's time. And there are many times when you will look at your family, your friends, your children and say 'Yes, I will give this to you, but not yet.' Because in my wisdom, I understand that there is something else you need to learn or put in place, and it is not simply an exercise in patience. It is an exercise in guidance, nurturing, and caring for and about you.

"So having said all that, what I wish to speak of is the Pink Diamond imbedded in your heart, even as we speak. It is the gift of being and anchoring in the fullness of your divinity in form on Earth. You have embraced divinity, and you have worked with the Masters, the Ascended Ones and I, but there has always been this small part of you that has held back. Child, there can be no more hanging back. That time is over.

"I have asked you to step forward, and you have done so in a whole variety of ways. Make no mistake about it, you have done well. You have done magnificently. You have cleared up the old debris, the issues that have haunted you, and you have been stepping forward. But now we are upping the ante.

"When I say you are bright angels in form, I am not simply speaking metaphorically. I am not speaking to merely give you compliments. Long before you lived on the distant planets of Arcturus or Cee Cee Cee or Electra, you have been angels. That is what I wish you to remember – not in some airy fairy way. For when you come to really know the angels, you will know there is nothing airy fairy about them. They are joyous, they are beautiful, and they are glorious. And they are serious, powerful, focused and mightily determined. You have seen this with your own guides. They do not give up on you. Sometimes you have given up on them, but they do not give up on you.

"The gift of the Pink Diamond is to ignite that perfection of your divinity. It is a state of being. And if you wish a tangible image then think of a Pink Diamond within your heart. It is a good place to put it and to think of it, because we will be working a lot. Make no error in your thinking – this is a state of being in the full divinity and the expression of that divinity, the beauty, grace, truth, and Love of who you are. Not who I am, but who you are. You are the teachers, you are the creators, you are the pathfinders, the healers, the channels. This is not a gift that I am bestowing freely upon the planet. It is not like my Blue Diamond that I have instilled upon the collective, so that they would begin to heal and know that they are Loved. This is a gift to you. It is the gift from the Father and I directly to your heart.

"Stay in that place of Love and to no longer, ever, vary from it. When you have received this light, when you have fully accepted it within, then anger and fear, disease, dread, these lesser human emotions, cannot co-exist. They are gone, and the sense of potential truly emerges.

"You ask of me 'Mother, how do you stay in Love when there is so much going on?' And I say to you, the more that is going on, the more urgent, the more important it is to stay in the Love. It is easy to stay in the Love when you are in a group of Lightholders. That is not the challenge. But child understand what we are telling you and that is by accepting this gift, it gives you that ability to stay in Love, in the divinity of your being.

"Now you say 'How does that work?' There are beings, some of which you can relate to and know, Mother Theresa, St. Francis of Assisi, Padre Pio, St. Theresa, the Buddha, Gandhi, who always remained in the Love, stayed within their Pink Diamond divinity. You say 'Well, I am not a saint.' And I suggest to you, get busy. You are underestimating yourself. Anyway, is saint not a funny little title to give somebody: you're a saint and you're not? It is absurd, isn't it?

"How you stay in the Pink Diamond divinity is by keep bringing yourself back to the Love. You never sit in judgment. You sit in discernment. You do not sit in fear or anger. You sit in Love, knowing that in that Love (and no it is not naïveté) in that Love there is a knowing of divine perfection, not only within you but within the multiverse.

"You say 'Well Mary, that's wonderful but other people aren't coming from that place.' Well, how will they ever get there if you are not transmitting it? I have said to you time and time again you are my pathfinders, you are my teachers, and you are the showers of the way. The angels of pink that surround you this day, they will not be swooping down and appearing to the multitude. Oh, they make their presence known but not in those kind of ways, for there would be far too many heart attacks. You dear hearts are the human transmitters, the beacons. So this transmission to the collective is your responsibility. Yes, I understand that this is term many of you shy away from; it is by a word that many of you do not like. Nevertheless, how you stay in the Love is by acceptance of that responsibility and discipline – practice. But it is not arduous practice.

"Now think about this for a moment, my children. You are sitting, and you are watching something that is highly disturbing, and so now you have a choice. Do you get angry and go into judgment or do you stay in Love? Now which one is going to make you feel better? Which one is going to have a clearer impact on the outcome whether it is war, a stubborn spouse, a nasty neighbor, or someone in the grocery store being obnoxious? When The Magdalena and I accompanied Jesus, Jeshua, my beloved son, we did not carry hatred and judgment for those who would betray him, or wish him dead because of political intrigue. That would have defeated the purpose. Was it easy? No.

"The element of being in your heart engenders compassion and forgiveness, forgiveness of yourself, forgiveness of others and sometimes forgiveness of us. That compassion is the ability to put yourself in somebody else's shoes and understand 'They're in a mess!' So what do you have to give them? Oh, you can give them wise words and counsel, but really all that, is Love. It is the substance of the Universe. It is absolutely the fuel that moves everything. It is the subatomic matter. And how you do it is by practice.

"And while I am asking you to stay in your heart, I also wish you to remember that you have been given this five-pointed star (a crown upon your forehead) for your wisdom vision, to truly be able to see what is transpiring in front of you, really what is unfolding. Not with the drama of I want, I need, I hope in a selfish way but to truly see so that you are looking with the eyes of Love from your third, fourth and actual eyes as well as your heart. Now understand, if you were not already mostly there, we would not be having this conversation. You are here because you are ready to do this.

"Let me be clear. This gift does not come with conditions. None of my gifts do. If you need assistance, then simply ask me. Ask Ariel, Archangel, and Queen of Pink. My desire and my request of each of you is not to lose your delightful personalities, not to destroy the ego for that is part of the delight of who you are – it is that expression of your divinity. So it is not about tapping down and practicing for sainthood. My beloved Padre Pio who sits with me now, he has encompassed it perfectly: pray, hope and don't worry. That is what I ask of you.

"Go with my Love. Go with my radiance of Pink Diamond. Sink now children into your heart. Close your eyes. Place your hands upon your heart. And receive. Enter into this state of being with me forever.

"Breathe and pause. Take a moment of silence my child.

"You will feel the Shifts and movement not only in your heart but in your being over the course of the next few days. Allow it to be. Again, go with my Love, infinite blessings and my infinite availability and help. Farewell."

You have just received the attunement of the gift of the Pink Diamond. You might want to take a break now and rest.

Universal Mother Mary has emphasized with us that it is very important to fully understand the qualities, vibration and power of the Pink Diamond energy.

She shares that the gifts of the Pink Diamond are "perfect clarity, perfect discernment, and unique courage. We have not spoken often about perfection, not because we shy away from it, but because you so often do. Yes, my beloved ones, you are an absolute work in progress, and you are perfect. You are perfection. And in this space, in this mirror of my Love, in the stillness of this place, I need you to know this. Your higher universal self, your higher self already knows this. I speak to the sweet human being; to your heart that you will also know you are divine perfection. It is not a matter 'If I do this, I will be better, I will be perfect.' We hear this so much, and it is erroneous. And not only that, it is sad because what you are doing is giving yourself false information and false messages. With this gift of clarity, with this gift of heart diamond, I wish you to discern the wisdom, the generosity, the beauty that lies within you, in perfection. That is not a matter of ego, my beloved ones. It is simply a matter of being. In perfection, there is humility."

Universal Mother Mary's 2010 New Year's gift was an expansion of the Pink Diamond energy, and, a deeper understanding of what it means to be in the state of grace, which is to be in a state of completion. This is crucial for our understanding of how to prepare for our Ascension. As the Mother reminds us, in order to ascend we need to be in that:

"State of grace is a place of wholeness, of connection, of reconnection, of reunion, of beauty, of laughter, of joy, of Love, of forgiveness, of compassion, of fortitude, of courage, and prudence. It is the culmination – let each moment be transformation. That is what I ask of you, for when you are the state of grace you are the transformation."

"My precious angels of Pink Diamond, what do I say to you on this graduation day? I tell you what I say: I tell you how proud I am, and it is with a Mother's pride, not about what I have accomplished but what you have accomplished. It is funny because within my realm, all is known and all is occurring, and yet still I am suggesting to you, I am telling you, that I am amazed at the progress you have made – each and every one of you. I have asked you to step forward each in your own very unique way, for that is the beauty of the plan, which is the beauty of the unfoldment. And you have done so.

"So what is missing? What is this next step about? It is about completion. And it is about being the state of grace. Now mark what I say, for I use my words and your language very particularly. I do not say being in the state of grace. I am asking and suggesting that you are the state of grace. That is the completion. That is the place of wholeness, of connection, of reconnection, of reunion, of beauty, of laughter, of joy, of Love, of forgiveness, of compassion, of fortitude and courage, of prudence. It is the culmination.

"You say 'Mary, are you telling me that the world or my life is coming to an end?' No, we are just getting started. But this is a new adventure. It is an invitation that I have extended to each one of your hearts, and you have answered. So often on Earth you pray, and I emphasize again how important prayer is. I like to talk with you. But you sometimes ask for answered prayers. Well, as strange as this may seem, so do we.

"I am the holder of hope. I am the receptacle of trust. But in that holding, do you not think that I hope as well, that I trust infinitely as well? If I did not have such Love, hope and trust in each and every one of you, we would not be sitting here talking about the unfoldment of my plan, of my plan of creation for this planet and for the angels that dance upon it and the angels that dance above it in these tubes called starships and these beings who dance in Middle Earth and protect the council fire, the heart of Gaia.

"The unfoldment of the plan is not just about me. That is not how I structured this creation. I can birth a planet with just you and I, and allow it to unfold and the creation to be complete. But that is not the nature of this creation. This creation is a co-creation with my beloved angels, with my very sweet human beings. If there is one consistent drawback in this collective, it is that you underestimate who you are and your role, your very pivotal part in this unfoldment of Love.

"Sometimes I listen to your prayers, and you say 'Mother, I am tired. Why is it so darn important that we do this Love thing? Couldn't you just have a plan somewhere else, and I could come home and help?' No. Now, if you exercise your free will and come home, would I embrace you? Would I welcome you? Would I shed tears of joy? Of course. But that is not the plan. The plan is to know and to be the experience of Love not only in physical form – and I know we have emphasized that a great deal because so many of you are ready to pop out of your physical form but it is not simply in the physical form – it is in all the forms and all the kingdoms. It is that unity on this beautiful, beautiful globe where the trees and the humans, the oceans and the sky, the devas (the guardians of the land) and the fairies, the rabbits and the lions are all singing and playing together.

"When we sit quietly together, you and I, and when you remember this, truly remember this, you go 'Oh yeah, I'll stay, I'll keep going.' And in that casual thought, you fill your Mother's heart. You fill my heart with pride and joy and such overflowing Love.

"The transformation, what you think of as the Shift or Ascension, is already rapidly underway – keep your eyes and ears open, each of you in a different way. This transformation is not just for me, although I know you would do it in praise and veneration for me. I know your heart. But it is also for you. It is for each and every one of you. And it is for all of you together as well. So when you return home, you can finally say 'Mother, we did it.' And then we'll sit and talk about what's next. Because although so often you say 'Never again,' I know you. You have the spirit of the adventurer, and you have enough Love to fill an entire galaxy. Do not ever question whether such a small group could change a planet. You have a mighty retinue, and it is already under way.

"I am not like my beloved son speaking of the future, although we are anxious. But in this time, let each moment be transformation. And if you don't know how that works, then ask me. Because sometimes the transformation is simply wrapping yourself in my cloak of blue, resting and refilling so that you are ready to go on. I don't want you dragging yourself bloody and bruised. That is not of Love. That is the last thing I would want. Sometimes the transformation is dancing and laughing. And other times, it is the serious conversations you have with each other or strangers when you say 'You know that isn't the way I think or feel.' It is when you prop each other up, it is when you beam through the supermarket or shine at dinner, when you compare notes. Each of these are moments of transformation. This is what I ask of you. When you are the state of grace, you are the transformation."

The Divine Mother also speaks to us about 2012 and the fact there is no need to wait to make our transition to the higher dimensional planes right now:

"You have much discussion on your planet about this wonderful date called 2012. I urge you do not get stuck on dates. For you can be that embodiment of Love right now, and I ask you: Why wouldn't you be? Why would you choose to wait? For when you wait, when you stall, when you hesitate, you slow down the process of conversion of the entire collective. You cannot wait on others to do what you are intended to do, what has always been part and parcel of your soul contract.

"I ask you to step forward, to move into the world, into the reality of Nova Earth and the higher dimensions. With this gift of my Pink Diamond, I ask you not only to be in the world but to be of the world and to carry the world, the planet, the collective, the kingdoms all within you, within your heart, you are fully capable of doing that. Expand your reality, child. You did not come to live in any form of limitation. That is a human belief system, and not even a useful one. Allow yourself to use the wings that have always been there. Fly free. Declare yourself. As you change, as you receive this gift of Pink Diamond, as you beam and share this gift with others, you will change your planet and yourself. Peace and creativity will reign. And people will know the truth of their hearts because it will be mirrored to them through yours.

"Your capacity for creation is infinite. It is time for you to realize that not only within your head but also deep within your heart and your cellular level, to accept the fullness and the wholeness of who you are. You are born from the heart of the Father and I. And you were born with the capacity not only to fulfill your desires but to create for Gaia and for the collective as well as your sweet self. It has never been an either/or. When you create for others, you are giving to your sacred self. And when you create for your sacred self, you are setting the energy for the collective, and you are acknowledging your place amongst all kingdoms, all realms in unity with Gaia."

The Universal Mother has been clear that the gift of the Pink Diamond has been and is bestowed selectively, not to the collective as a whole. The catch in that is that she has entrusted us with the task of transmitting this incredible gift to others, to the collective. It has never been the Divine intention that the gift not be shared. Mary directs us in this undertaking as well.

"As you change, as you receive this gift, as you beam and share this gift with others, you will change your planet. And peace and creativity will reign. People will know the truth of their hearts because it will be mirrored to them through yours." So beam away – but remember you are going to be beaming from the fifth or the seventh into the third.

This section begins with one of the most beautiful channelings ever from the Universal Mother on the Pink Diamond. She speaks of it as giving us the gift of who we are. Can you imagine a gift of greater Love?

"I bring you my joyous gift of Pink Diamond this day. Child, I do not bring this gift forward casually –joyfully yes, but not casually. This gift comes from my heart where I have stored it for you awaiting your readiness. This is the gift of your own sacred divinity, your wholeness, your essence and your expression within this lifetime and all time, all realities, all dimensions, all universes. For do we not live in an omniverse? We want you to begin to understand that more clearly.

"There is and there can be no separation. My Love for you is infinite. But, dear hearts, it is also time for you to know, to acknowledge, and to receive your own divinity. I do not bestow grace upon you, although I would gladly do so. I wish you to awaken, sweet angels, to the immutable fact, that you are grace. This is the gift of the Pink Diamond. This is the gift of who you are. Grace incorporates all blessings, all virtues.

"What do I mean by that? What I mean is you have absolutely everything, not only what you need or require to complete your mission. And do not forget the first part of your mission, the first part of your sacred contract is to be an angel in form, experiencing joy. You cannot live, or be, or extend in service if you are not in the joy, if you are not in the Love, if you are not accepting completely, deeply, wholly and holy that you are Love. That is all you have ever been.

"There have been many adventures and, yes, some misadventures, but that does not change or alter the infinite essence of who you are. I give you this gift of Pink Diamond to awaken you – not that you will step into the next unfoldment but that you will run, jump, hopscotch into the unity of your next step and the next step of those this circle with you.

"Dear heart, you are emotional beings, and it is part of that to laugh, to cry, to feel. Many of you have forgotten this in your clearing and in your removal of old debris. Yes, joy and Love are a state of being, but they also express as emotions; and they raise your frequency and vibration more than you will ever know. It was desirable and necessary to let go of fear, anger, frustration, judgment, but do not let go of the plethora of other emotions that are within you. That is the human experience and that is Nova Being.

"I bless you. This gift will continue to expand and my request of you is to allow this to happen. Understand what I say. There is no limitation to the expansion of your Pink Diamond. You are an infinite being with infinite potential to create. That is the way that I have birthed you, so do not forget that. Go with my Love. Farewell."

We conclude this section by a channeling with the Universal Mother in which she reminds us not only to allow the Pink Radiance of our being to expand, but to remember the importance of completion in all of our creations and undertakings.

"Greetings, I am Mary, Universal Mother, Mother of Hope and Mother of Love, and Mother of each of you, my rainbow angels, my creation angels of Light. I welcome you, and I remind you once again of the wondrous Pink, the diamond that I place in your heart, in your mind, in your field, in your body, in your life, in every aspect of you, wherever and however you are. I remind you of this because it is the wholeness of who you are.

"I speak to you about the power of completion. For what you do in your life, and even on our side what we do, requires a beginning, middle and end. Completion is necessary to begin again. At each stage of your creation there is completion. You do not start a prayer and never finish it. You do not go to the still-point and hold it for eternity. You do not go into action, and keep going and keep going. Completion is an essential part of creation and of each and everything you do, particularly while in human form.

"There is a habit, and we would even say a human addiction, for many to start something and never complete it. This is not judgment and certainly not criticism. It is said in order to assist you because in completion the fullness of what you have created comes forward. Part of completion is letting go, of trusting, allowing and knowing that you have done what you intended to do, and, you have done it to the best of your ability. I do not just mean your physical ability or your mental ability – I mean the expanded totality of your Pink Radiance. It is the knowing that when you have completed it, that you basically are handing it over for delivery. You are handing it over to the Father, to me, to Jeshua, to Gabrielle. You are handing it over and saying 'Alright, I have done my part. I am holding the space within my heart. Now it is up to you.' It is the sacred partnership that we have entered eons ago. We will fulfill our promise. We will fulfill our part of this sacred vow of co-creation with you.

"Long ago, when each of you were considering this return to Earth during this critical time of the fulfillment and unfoldment of my plan, you said to me, 'Mother, of course, I will go. I will do anything to help and to serve thee." But you also said to me, "Mother, how will I know, how will I know when it is done? How will I know when I can set it aside, and I have done everything?' And I said to you, dear hearts, stop before the point of exhaustion.

"Yes, there are times when it is necessary to push through something. But that is not the energy of creation. The energy of creation is light and airy. It is taking energy codes, gathering them out of thin air and allowing them to formulate into what your heart desires, because what your heart desires is in perfect alignment with our plan. So when you feel that sense of peace, and that is well before exhaustion, stop. Hand it to me. Hand it to Gabrielle. Hand it to Jophiel. Hand it over to your beloved guides. And then allow. Open your arms, your heart and your being, and simply allow. Allow yourself to receive, and to trust us. We are not in the habit of ever letting you down. When you have committed your heart to our sacred partnership to create what your heart desires, we have agreed to assist thee. You have asked, and we promise, you will receive. It is the nature of our agreement. And it is the fulfillment of our Love."

So to sum up, what are the unique aspects of the Pink Diamond energy? It is the ignition of your perfection of divinity. It is a state of being in your full divinity and the expression of that divinity, the beauty, grace, truth, and Love of who you are. The qualities of the Pink Diamond energy imbedded with you are perfect clarity, perfect discernment, unique courage, wisdom, independence, beauty and being grace. The gift of this energy acts as a balancer, unifier, harmonizer, and promotes focus and determination. What could be better, more sacred than that? The Tri-Flame, is what so read on.

Chapter 7

Yahweh's Golden Flame

There comes a time in each of our lives when we are ready and willing to accept the energy of the Father in a balanced, welcoming, nurturing manner. For each of us the father journey has been individual, depending on our culture, family, and of course the personal dynamic between our fathers and ourselves. For some the experience has been wonderful, for others a living nightmare. Even others had no father presence and which leaves an indelible impression on how you perceive that energy.

My family would likely agree that I was my father's favorite. I know parents aren't to have favorites, but invariably they do and we all perceive it. This mild favoritism was a double-edged sword because it did not give me license. Quite the contrary. At a very early age I learned to "dance on a dime" as I put it years later in therapy. I always wanted to live up to the dreams and expectations of my parents, never to disappoint my dad. I share this personal experience to highlight that each of us comes to a point when we have to look in the mirror and let that human experience go. But what I have often witnessed is that in doing so we let go of the father energy – or distance ourselves from it in order to obtain and maintain our independence. If we are lucky, we know somewhere in the background, dad is still there just in case. But all too often in this process we distance ourselves from the Divine Father energy as well.

The Divine Mother energy is predictable – nurturing and forgiving. We expect that and always receive it in abundance. But the Father energy is different. Even if we have long gotten past the misconceptions of the punishing, thundering God of the Old Testament, it's still a collective memory. Sadly, that sense of stand back and be respectful is all too often present.

One of the most significant shifts in the energy changes of the past few years is the return of the Divine Father in our hearts, minds, and beings. It is the warm, loving Father who is here to help us, to teach us the "family business," to shelter us when we are emotionally, spiritually or physically cold, and to protect us because we are our loved deeply and forever.

For many years the Divine Father or Divine Masculine energy of the Mother/Father/One was almost silent, present but not primary. For many people, feelings regarding the energies of the Divine Father have been reflected through the old lenses of the punishing angry patriarch. That has never been the energy of the Father that I have experienced through the Council of Love. Quite the contrary.

The first time the Council channeled the Thirteenth Octave meditation and I landed in the lap of the Father I felt that I was finally home. I was in a place of such tender caring that I never wanted to leave. The quiet strength and boundless Love and honoring that you feel in connecting with this energy not only fills you; but makes you acknowledge your heritage, the truth of who you are, and what you are truly capable of being.

Nevertheless, for years in the work with the Council, Yahweh stood back, ever-present but more the observer than the participant – the "hands-off father" as it were, that is until we began our creation work. Then Yahweh stepped up front and center. He has gifted us with the keys to the Warehouse of Heaven, he guides us in how to work with the creation codes of Love, he protects us while encouraging us to go forward, expand and stretch our wings. He is there for us, actively, in awesome ways.

Full partnership, co-creation and paradigm shift are the key elements of the Ascension process or the Shift. This is where Yahweh truly steps forward and fully expresses his relationship with and to us. For that reason I include the following channelings because it's important for each of you to feel the immense Love of our Father, and to cleanse any of those old images prior to fully receiving the gift of his Golden Flame. As you read allow the energy of Yahweh, which is imbedded not only in these words but in the space in between the words and letters, to fill your heart and infuse you with his golden essence. Allow the Love the Father has always had for you to seep gently into you and fill every pore of your essence.

The Father's Request

"Greetings, I am Yahweh, Father God, Father. Finally, we are all ready to simply sit down and have this conversation as Father and daughter/son. I thank you. Come and be with me as I have always been and will always be with you in and out of form in a wide variety of places and forms.

"I only have one request of you, and it is a Father's request: let me spoil you. Let me spoil you, not because I think that you are in any way incompetent but rather because I am so proud of you. I know your capacities. I know your wholeness. I know your abilities to walk the Earth and far beyond and bring forward what you desire. I know this.

"It is not unusual that a Father's prerogative is to simply bestow upon his loved ones, his children what he has available to him. So I give you my infinite Love, my infinite Wisdom, my infinite Will. Take from the Warehouse of Heaven whatever you want. It's yours. It always has been. And if you really want, I'll set up a delivery system, and that way you won't have to be confused. You can order up whatever you want, and Uriel will help me and deliver it right to your heart from mine.

"When we began this, when the Mother said to me 'It is time to give my children the Pink Diamond,' I trusted her. I always do. You have taken this gift and you have anchored it in your hearts. You have expanded your sacred being far beyond what either one of us anticipated. The rate at which you are growing is a miracle for us to behold.

"Never, never doubt yourselves. It does not matter, my sweet angels, if you can dance and tap your fingers. It does not matter if you do not see or hear because you do in your heart. It is the

Love that counts. It is the Love that is the fuel of everything – everything.

Never think that you are less than perfect. I won't hear of it. If there is any hesitation, any small gap, turn to me. I am right here. I am right here with you. I am not a distant Father, far away in another Universe. I am right here talking to you, my sons and daughters. I Love you. Farewell."

Yahweh on Creation

"Greetings, I am Yahweh, Universal Father, Father of the Universe, Creator. I do not come to simply speak as distant Source or friend. I come to speak and to embrace you, my beloved ones, as children of my heart. For as the Mother and I are united as one, so are you. And in very practical terms, I want to speak to you about what this means.

"Each of you has had a variety of experiences with parental figures, especially father figures, and the fathers that you have chosen and who have chosen you to travel with during this lifetime. Some of your experience has been wonderful, loving and kind; respectful and honoring. For some of you, it has been mediocre. For others it has been a walk in terror. And often you have asked me through this channel, 'Why did I make that choice?' And, of course, you made it to be a vessel of Love. You made it so that you would be an anchor of Love in that family. Never does one choose parents and come into a physical situation anticipating that you will not be loved and nurtured, that you will not be tended to emotionally, physically and spiritually.

"But throughout all of those experiences, my beloved ones, the immutable fact remains: I am your Father just as Mary is your Mother. There are so many times when I feel you shy away from that. I understand about independence, choice and the growth of spirit whether it is in form or even on this side. But I wish this union and unity between us to be much stronger. I wish it to be the relationship that cherishes and warms you in the darkest hour and the relationship that you share in the most shining of glorious moments. I wish to teach you what you need to know to walk your dream and your fulfillment upon this planet and this sojourn on Earth.

"Year and years ago, I invited you into the family business, thinking that this was a language that you would understand and embrace. For our family business is creation and Love. We are manufacturers, my friends. We manufacture all kinds of creations, things that you know upon Earth and things that you have never even dreamed of. The material that we manufacture with is Love. And we do so in unity and in joy. And so I repeatedly ask you to come with me, come with me to the factory or to the warehouse where we will go and access the creation codes. Where we will gather once again the molecules of Love, the subatomic particles of Love, and then manipulate them and Love them into form.

"Now I am talking as a very practical Father this day. So I am not talking merely exclusively, shall I say, about creating those qualities that you wish to see upon the planet, that we all wish to see upon the planet. I am not just talking about peace or patience or stamina. I am also talking to you about the practicalities of your life. What is it, my beloved one, which you wish to manufacture, bring into form in your life? How are we going to work together and transmute this energy of the Universe and package it into what your heart desires. It can be a book, a healing practice, a life free of financial duress.

"I do not mean that we are manufacturing the ability for you to hold energy – you already have that. I am talking about the bricks and mortar, people walking through the door. Is it a mate? Is it a mate of flesh and blood? I am not suggesting that we are going to build him or her, but we will create the energy field that will draw that person immediately to you. Don't forget I have invited you to access the Warehouse of Heaven with me or even without me. But as your Father, as one who Loves you so deeply, I want to accompany you until you have the knack, until you really understand in very human practical terms how to do this.

"The Council of Love has given you the theory of how to create, the formulas, the how-to, and yet you are still not creating to the magnitude that we wish to see. Let us be clear: we wish to see it not only for you, but for the planet. Because once you have the knack of this, you are not going to stop. You're going to keep going, and you will be creating for the collective and for the planet.

"Yes, I urge you: take care of yourself first. When you are flying in one of Raphael's planes, we say put the air mask on yourself first and then turn to others. Well, that is my advice as well. Let us tend to your sacred garden, the garden of your heart and your soul; your emotional being and your delightful ego. And from there let us expand. Then if you wish to specialize I would be happy and honored to help you do so. If your goal is that you wish to create homes for humanity, then I will help you. If you wish to write books and not just write them but publish them, if you wish to sing and have a hit song, I will help you. I am trying to cover the range that you will understand the magnitude of what I am offering. Please come with me.

"Part of your divinity, part of assuming the miraculous gift of the Mother is this gift of your divinity in form in this time of Ascension, of magnificent rebirth and building of Nova Earth. But it is also energy that is involved in stepping forward and creating, and that is why I am talking to you about this right now. So the question is what do you wish to create? You have been given the energy, the totality of your expression of us, not esoterically, not spiritually, but physically as well.

"Your world is becoming a gentler place second by second, millisecond by millisecond. And, yes, I understand time. So what are you going to do with it? If there is the slightest hesitation of 'Well, oh gee, I'm just not sure Dad. I'm not sure what it is I want to do, what business I want to create or what conglomerate I want to create,' then let me help you. Let us all help you. This Council of Love is exactly what its name implies. It is our expression of unity and community. And you are part of this Council. You declared yourself part of it a long time ago.

"Please come with me. Let my gold warm you. Let my Love warm you. I am not an old man sitting on a mountaintop in judgment. I am the Father sitting next to you with my hand on your shoulder simply saying 'how can I help?' And when I'm saying this, I'm not saying 'let me do it for you.' You have grown out of that. It would not be respectful of me to say that to you now. But there are pieces perhaps that are not clear to you, parts that are not fully available to you.

"I am with you. This is the time of creation and co-creation. The codes are within you and around you. Gather them and call on me. Go with my Love. Go with my laughter, my joy, for this is intended to be fun. Think of it that way. When we created the multiverse, we did not sit with furrowed brows agonizing over what to do. We did it with delight and joy. That is how creation takes place. It is ecstatic work. It is bliss."

It wasn't until the Sedona Annual Gathering in 2011 that our Divine Father blessed us with his Golden Flame, his essence of wholeness, the essence of the Divine Masculine. This attunement is the gift, of the essence of the Divine Masculine, the union with the Father, with the ability to co-create and anchor in physicality upon Earth.

Yahweh speaks to our hearts when He says: "I give you my Golden Flame, the flame of Infinite Creation, my essence to balance with the Mothers and with yours. I give you my essence to balance the male and female, the divine masculine and feminine. I give it to you that you may jump forward not only in time but in joy, in glee, in courage, in faith, and in action.

"There is much talk upon your planet these days about Ascension. The Ascension is simply a higher realm of consciousness, a higher realm of being – so as I instill this Golden Flame within you, I ignite that higher knowing. I give this to you from my heart to yours because you are loved and you are cherished, and I am your Father."

Yahweh's Gift of the Golden Flame, Conscious Creation, and Ascension

"Greetings, I am Yahweh, Father, Source, Creator, Eternal Flame of Love, Eternal Creator. Welcome my children, my children of my heart and soul. Welcome to this time and this process of creation.

"You have all you need within your being to go forward in your creation and in the creation of Cities of Light, Nova Earth and Nova Being. But nevertheless, I wish to give to you my essence, the Golden Flame. The Mother has gifted you with her Blue Diamond long ago. You have integrated the Pink Diamond of your sweet wholeness. I wish to complete that triad for we are in the unity of One. We have been in the unity of One for a long time. We return there every time you enter into the Thirteenth Octave.

"Often, what is missing in your creation work is you stepping forward in actions aligned to bring forth what you desire. You need to literally grab hold and claim as your birthright what has always been yours. This is not a matter of greed; that is a human judgment and invention. Creation is infinite and eternal, it never stops or ceases, so it is simply time for you to join in. You have done so your entire life in various ways. Now what you are doing is bringing it to conscious awareness, and you do so as part of the evolution of the collective, as well as part of your own evolution."

Yahweh further explains and blesses us with a deeper understanding of his Golden Flame, which is the flame of infinite knowledge, of infinite creation, and infinite understanding of the creation codes.

"Greetings, I AM Yahweh. Welcome, welcome my beloved children of every ray, of every color, of every pathway, of every reality. You do not beckon to me often although I am ever-present in your life, in your field, within this Universe.

"I do not step forward unless you request my presence. I want none to believe or think that I in any way wish to interfere. Quite the contrary, for I have stood back for eons and watched with trust, awe and faith and yes, my beloved ones, great joy. I have watched your unfoldment, your evolution, your moving forward. I have watched the progression of both you and the collective, particularly those who inhabit the planet of Earth, of

Terra Nova, at this time, because it is a time of great change, and, a time of the completion. This era of completion began many years ago. But unless it is within a very short time-span, many of you do not realize that you are in a process of completion, as is Gaia, as are we, in this unfoldment, and the renewal of the plan of the beloved Mother upon this planet.

"But that is not what I wish to speak to you about this day, what I wish to speak to you and to remind you of and to re-instill within your heart is my Golden Flame. It is the Golden Flame of Divine Masculine. It is the third point in your precious Tri-Flame. And you say to me 'yes, oh yes, I forgot about that, thank you Father.'

"I wish to speak to you about this Golden Flame, this gift that I bestow upon you freely and lovingly. In some ways, the Golden Flame is the flame of completion. You have the Blue Diamond and the Pink, but the Gold is integral too. Without it you are lop-sided, you are incomplete. And it is a time upon Gaia when not only do you wish to be firmly grounded and anchored within her being, you do most certainly do not wish to walk around lop-sided.

"The Golden Flame is the gift of my essence. It is not some-thing that I have created in my infinite Universe that is external to me. Just like the Blue Diamond, it is my core and my essence that I gift to you today and that I re-ignite within you again today. It is the energy of the Divine Masculine, the balancer, but it is also the flame of infinite knowledge, of infinite creation, of infinite understanding of the creation codes. It is the Golden Flame of inspiration and my beloved ones it is the Golden Flame of action.

"Most of the time this Golden Flame, this energy that I instill so brightly within each of your hearts, is used internally. It is not something that you are extending out into the Universe except under very particular circumstances. You are using it within, burning brightly, to allow you to see what energies you have need to bring forward to create exactly what you want and de-sire.

"Every day the Mother and I sit here and listen to each of

you. We wonder at your plea to us when you say 'Why have things not happened? Why has this not transpired? Why does this not come forth?' And then we look at each other and think 'why are they not using the gifts of creation that they have been given?'

"We have entered into a very equal partnership of family, and as our beloved child, whether you are 90 or nine, we have given you everything. The Golden Flame is to remind you of that. You have no need to seek in any way external from yourself. The Golden Flame is a torch that can show you the way back to my Warehouse of Heaven, which very few of you have ever visited since our first encounter. I wonder why, when I have opened the doors and invited you in to come and to take freely everything. Not only what your heart desires, but what you believe you need for the completion of this journey, for the completion of your role upon Terra Gaia, the completion of what you wish to do, not only in terms of your mission but for the sheer fun of it. You can as easily create a bicycle or a Ferris wheel; it does not need to be practical, in fact quite the contrary.

"When you sit, whether it is in quiet contemplation or in meditation, and ask 'What do I need to know? What do I need to know to heal this situation, to go forward, to address it, just to live my life?' I guide you, use the Golden Flame. See yourself within your heart encompassed in my Golden Flame; the knowledge is there and next to the knowledge is the inspiration that will spur you on. Then move into the action because dear hearts now is a time of action. You have had the time of clearing, you have had the time of expanding your energy field, you have had the time of learning, and of magnificently incorporating the energies that we have sent to this Earth plane.

"Now you need to move, with everything you know, have learned and done, into the time of action. Action may simply be claiming your place within the Shift. Since the very first day this Council has addressed you, we have addressed you as pathfinders and showers of the way. This is not simply a phrase or an accolade; it is information about who you are. But how my beloved ones can you be a way shower or a pathfinder if you are not moving into action?

"Let me be clear about this, the first actions are internal; you will not walk the street carrying my Golden Flame, it is internal and it will show you the way. I will show you the way, I will lift you up and position you, I will point, I will back you up, and I will give you the resources you need.

"However, I will not do it for you because that is not the partnership that is not the contract, it is not the agreement. Will I lift you up if you are placing yourself in harm's way, if you are facing the wrong way? Yes I will, always. However, it is time for you, during this phase of completion, to fully enjoy and claim what you are capable of, as teacher, as healer, as friend, as mother, as brother. We are not just talking about what you do in the so-called world of work, for that is such a small percentage of who you are.

"Begin within, and when the action is decided upon, let it emerge to your outer world. It may emerge as just a smile, of looking someone directly in the eyes and smiling and sending them the two fingers to the heart in the grocery store. It may be being completely honest and forthright when someone says 'Well, what do you think?' Too often there is an 'I don't know' or the quiet conversation inside says 'if I told you what I really think you would run the other way.' Be brave, you have the golden courage, you have the Mighty Ones (the Archangels) always in attendance. Bring forth your Divine Masculine, not the bully, not the braggart, but the leader, the shower of the way.

"The Mother and I have gifted you with our very essence. We have invited you home to the Thirteenth Octave forever, and it is from this place that you ascend. So come and join with us every day in this place of Divine Union and from there, anchored firmly in the Thirteenth, float back down to the seventh, the fifth if you must, and then reach into the third, but do not pretend with this bright Tri-Flame that you live there anymore."

What Yahweh is really talking about is the sacred partnership and Love of family. He wants us to know that not only has He given us his core essence but that He is there for us in every conceivable way. It seems fitting therefore to conclude this section with a final message from Yahweh on the nature of that sacred partnership:

"I speak to you from my heart to your heart, from my will to your will, from my mind to your mind. And I will ask you what I have been asking this channel: do you Love me? Do you Love me?

"Understand we are a unified field of One, and that is why I have started this day by reminding you that I AM, that I AM all things, all energy, all Love. And while I often have spoken and do speak to you as your beloved Father, as the divine aspect of masculinity, to remind you that you receive your Father's Love and care – for this appears to be an issue for many, or so the channel tells me, and I tease her because I know it is so – I AM of Love and I AM Love.

"It is not conceivable; it is not possible that I do not care for you. Do not think if you are not receiving in exactly the way that you have asked, imagined or envisioned that it is because I do not care. That is not so. Let me suggest to you that the Mother and I are simply improving, adding, perfecting, expanding or aligning your creation or your plan. Because we know that your heart is pure and that the core of you, the soul of you, the God-self of you wishes to be in alignment with All. Gone are the days when you are simply working through or attempting to be in that alignment. That is over. It is no longer a matter of trying.

"Yes there are times when you relinquish or surrender what you are creating to us, and we are doing our bit as well. Yes, you are mighty creator, but you are mighty creator because you also participate in this Presence, in the unity of our heart, our mind, our will, our Love. And, yes, there are sometimes elements that we are adding to the creation or the plan – not to shift what you have called forth but to perhaps add to what you might have overlooked or did not understand was an element in the creation because you do not always have the full picture of creation, of the infinity of the Universe, of the omniverse. This is not criticism. This is partnership, and it is the most sacred partnership that we enter into with you.

"I want to tell you, to remind you, there is never, never a

whispered prayer that is not heard and acted upon. There is never an intent that you hold in the stillpoint that we do not conjoin with to add our energy and to bring forth – that is where we do the joining and the alignment. There is not an action that you take in your physical realm that is not in alignment with the wisdom of All.

"So when I ask you, my beloved one, 'do you Love me?' I am not coming to you as a needy partner, as a child wondering or as a parent needing reassurance. It is because, if you Love me, and I know you do, then you must Love yourself. It is a statement of reality that cannot be escaped. You are part of the I AM. You are part of All. You're a part of the unified force field. You are part of me as I am part of you.

"There has been much misinformation or skewed information that has been communicated over the years in various religious followings, but the truth that you are created as part of me, as part of all of creation in the image and likeness, the child of One is the indelible truth. I suggest to you, my friends that you have the wisdom to know that truth, to know who you really are. And in that, to honor and to Love your sacred self exactly the way you Love us – nothing else makes sense. You cannot be in alignment with our mind and will and heart and be anything else. So I want you to feel and think of this as you go forward in this journey and in this time of tremendous opening on every single level above and below.

"There has never been a time of such open creation upon this planet, not even in the time of Lemuria and Atlantis. When you are in your heart and mind and will, remember the Love. Remember the Love not only that we have for you and that you have for us and that we share, but remember the honoring and the Love that you are, that is your very fiber. Love, cherish, honor, respect, nurture, and care for your sweet self. And then with me declare "I AM."

The last meditation prior to the re-ignition of our Tri-Flame for the Ascension meditation and attunement comes from Yahweh, in a heart rending appeal to embrace his Golden Flame. We finish this section with this loving message:

"Yet again I give you my Golden Flame of Divine Masculine, of Love, of freedom and wisdom. Yes we differ and yet we are one, we are in the unity of One, we always have been. So sometimes you will think my flame looks like a diamond and that is just fine because the Mother is a flame as well, and so are you. It is the flame of empowerment, it is the flame of unfoldment, it is the flame of action, and it is the flame to be able to complete what you came here to do. And I will back you every step of the way. You are born of my heart, of the deepest Love, and when I gaze upon you I turn to the Mother and wonder, in awe, for I know what you are capable of creating and I know what you have already created. I am a proud father in many ways. But I ask to be the father of your heart, I ask you to turn to me as well, I ask you to walk with me. I Love you. I Love you forever. So let us create the unity of this Tri-Flame, let us recreate more clearly, more powerfully than ever what has always been within you. We are simply re-awakening and yes refilling. Let us begin."

Chapter 8 – Activation of the

Tri-Flame & The Sacred Heart of Jesus

The activation of the Golden Flame in 2010 set the stage for the completion of the activation and attunement of our heart's Tri-Flame. The instillation of the Golden Flame completes the triad with the Blue Diamond, the essence of Mother Mary, and the Pink Diamond, the essence of your sweet wholeness.

Universal Mother Mary reminds us:

"Do not forget to work with the Tri-Flame within your heart; the blue of the Mother, the pink of your divine self, and the gold of Yahweh's essence. Balance this and let it burn brightly, for it is what holds you in that place of clarity."

Little did we fully comprehend that when the activation of the unified Tri-Flame of our hearts was bestowed we were being given one of the key components for our Ascension. The Tri-Flame of Gaia has burned brightly for eons – that is one of the reasons why, when we anchor ourselves deep in her heart, it heals and fills us. It makes sense that in order to travel with Gaia, and all of the Mother's creations, up the golden spiral to the higher dimensions, we have to anchor our Tri-Flame deep within our hearts. Otherwise, we cannot experience the energy of the higher realms. We need to continually anchor that energy to ensure that it is burning brightly, and balanced, every day.

The watchword for our Ascension is balance. If we are not in balance, if we are not anchored in the heart of Gaia, if our male, female and divine self are not equally balanced then we cannot gracefully ascend through the golden spiral either now, or later.

Remember that Yahweh and the Universal Mother have told

us the energies of each of these flames, the blue, the pink and the gold, can take on many forms, such as diamonds, as roses, or sheer energy. Their ability to morph into useful and fulfilling forms is instantaneous and infinite. It is with that thought I invite you to receive the activation of the sacred Tri-Flame of your heart.

Be gentle with yourself, and make sure that you take time to rest and integrate after this meditation.

Activating the Heart Tri-Flame

Begin by taking a nice deep breath of pink, that beautiful Pink Diamond. Sink and anchor into your heart and relax, bringing yourself towards the end of the day and feeling that kind of gentle glow that you do when the sunset touches your face in that golden time. Feel your shoulders relax, your body become heavier as you sink into the chair.

Now, take a deep breathe of the Universal Mother's Blue Diamond, in through your nose and exhaling through your mouth. Feel that sparkly blue energy fill you – and relax.

Pause and breathe.

Now, another breath of Yahweh's Gold. Deeper. Feel the flame of God's protection, of His Love.

And now back to the beautiful Pink Diamond of your wholeness, of your divinity, which is extraordinarily bright. In…. and exhale.

Pause and breathe.

With me drop down deeper into your heart, into the center of your Tri-Flame which is located in the middle of your heart. Feel yourself sink into this energy center, not pushing just floating and observing, just being.

I want you to see and to feel and to experience the most beautiful pink rose that you have ever seen or smelled or sensed. It is a pink rose that isn't fully open yet. The bud is just beginning to blossom and it's that soft, gentle sweetheart rose. And feel the soft velvet of those petals and smell that damp fragrant freshness. Take a nice deep breath of that pink, in through your nose, out through your mouth, and go deeper. Feel all your energy, all the Love of who you are centered in that pink radiance. And really feel it.

It is the Mother's request that for this meditation we first visualize our Tri-Flame as roses. There are three roses. There is your masculine self and your feminine self, and the center of your brilliant wholeness. Now we will bring each of these aspects into perfect balance.

Stay in the center of your heart and see the perfect pink rose that rests there and inhale the subtle sweet fragrance, and feel the rich plush velvet petals. So see your pink rose, see all the glistening dew drops on it, all the sparkles of the Mother's Diamonds. And go into that rose, deeper, with the totality of your being. Feel the strength of the stem. This is your wholeness. This is the realization of your anchoring of your entirety, of your divinity, not just in a spiritual way but in a way of wholeness and physicality.

Pause and breathe.

Now ever so gently, look to the right in your heart and to see what rose lies there. Is it the golden rose of Yahweh? Maybe it's a purple rose. But this is a rose not of one of the Ascended Ones, but of you, of a part of your sweet self. So take a moment and feel, look, perceive. What is that rose that rests next to your pink in the center of your heart on the right?

Bring in the essence of that scent – the strength and the wisdom and whatever qualities this rose is carrying for you, so it is not prescribed. Take time and go into that rose and feel what it brings you. What is this masculine part of your being? Is it a strong and thorny rose? Does it hurt when you touch it? Is it weak looking and half dead because you've ignored it? If so, reinvigorate it. Share the dewdrops from your pink, and make it vital and healthy. Do not forget to reinforce and feed the stem of your sacred rose – it is vital. Feel the qualities of this beautiful rose. Become comfortable with it. Discover what you love about this rose, this part of yourself. And thank it for being part of you.

Pause and breathe.

Now go back to your center, to your pink. Rest and enjoy the dewy softness of your pink sweetheart rose, again feeling the strength of that stem – that connection to life-force.

Now go to the left, to the beautiful feminine rose that is sitting on the left hand side of your Tri-Flame roses, and breathe it in. You are not restricted to certain colors or rays. I want you to feel and to look and to sense what color, what energy is this rose on the left hand side of your heart. What does she look like? Is she strong and vibrant or is she withering? And if she is, reinforce her. Find out what you Love about her. Feel the strength of her stem. Explore every part of your rose. Feel her magic and her sense of indescribable hope.

Pause and breathe.

Now once again come back to your pink in the center of your heart.

I want you to turn to each side, to your right and to your left, and hear the prayer, the heartfelt request from each side of you; from each of your roses.

What does your feminine want you to do? What is the gift that it has been waiting for? For even if you feel that you are in the balance of your feminine, there is always further to go. There is always more to learn, to experience, to grow, to expand. So listen very carefully and receive that information with an open heart. What does she want?

Now turn to your right, to your masculine, and ask him the same thing. What is the heartfelt request and desire? What is the acknowledgment needed of your masculine self? Gently open and breathe and receive the messages and information. You can do this – just allow.

Pause and breathe.

Now, bring those messages and requests from your male and female back into the center.

You have learned from the Mother and Father that there can be no separation. These three roses, these three flames serve you incredibly well – each distinct, useful, powerful and wonderful in their own right – so you don't want to merge them. And yet you know in that very core of you that there needs to be that unity, connectedness and balance, each honored and represented equally, not only within your heart but within your life, within your physicality.

Take a moment and ensure as these roses are blossoming that they're equal, that they're equal in size and fragrance and vibration. Let them blossom in your heart right now. Let them fill you.

Pause and breathe.

Now take the stems, take the stems of these precious roses and feel them come out the back of your heart as you begin to braid them. Feel or sense them begin to intertwine and interweave themselves into one singular braid down your central column. See them turning into filaments of light. They are brilliant!

Your male and your female are equally sharing the divinity of your sacred space. Bring that braid all the way down to the tip of your tailbone, further – like your strands of DNA. And feel them join that kundalini energy, that flame at the base of your spine. Feel yourself heating up.

Pause and breathe. Take a moment and let that ignition happen.

Now bring all your energy to your third eye. And, with that kundalini energy, I want you to rise, pull it up – that woven strand of three, that braid, that filament of light – pull it up right to your third eye. Warmer and warmer, come on.

Breathe.

Breathe the colors of your flames, of your roses. Breathe and bring it to your third eye in the center of your forehead. Feel yourself get warmer.

Now bring that energy – that braid of Tri-Flame up to your crown, up to the very crown, pull it right up your central channel, up, out of your crown, pull up your filaments with the kundalini, pull it up. It's as simple as that – just pull it up. Like the temperature on a thermometer going up to your crown. Let's go.

Feel that blending of energies, a spiral of light. Open.

Pause and breathe.

Now bring it back into your heart. Bring it, pull it gently down again from your crown, back into that Tri-Flame that is unique to you, balanced and acknowledged, and so welcome.

Pause and breathe.

Now with your pink in the middle, I want you to switch sides. I want you to feel your masculine moving to the left and your feminine dancing to the right. And back again. Feel the integrity of the balance of honoring both sides, all parts of yourself, knowing that each plays a role and a critical role, a pivotal role.

And I want you to Love all three parts. Tell it. And agree that you will do what they have asked you to do.

Feeling that perfect bouquet that is unique to you, like no one else in the universe has, give thanks, deep gratitude for this perfect balance of your unique Tri-Flame.

Then when you're ready, come back and we'll continue.

Now that you have received the activation and attunement of your Tri-Flame, understand that you can build this energy through daily meditation. The more frequently you invoke and connect with this energy the stronger and more balanced you will become. If you are having a difficult day, or if you are having a particularly great one, then return to this sense of deep connection and awareness and allow the divinity of the feminine, masculine and your sweet wholeness to refresh your soul and your entire being.

In a channeling Mother Mary shared her insights into this process of the Tri-Flame initiation.

"Greetings, I am Mary, Universal Mother, Mother of Love and Mother of hope, Mother of change, Mother of creation, Mother of One. Oh, my beloved children, I am so proud of you!

"It is time for these illusions of distance to be eradicated, and I am so pleased that you have agreed to join with me now in Love.

"You have begun your journey as a spark of light – brilliant and illuminated. If you were to gaze at me in the same light and with the same Love that I gaze at you, you would see the brilliance of my essence; of my Blue Diamond; of my core; of all of the Divine Feminine. I have many faces and you have seen them all. My heart, my soul, my core, my essence is blue. I am filled with magnificent light and many facets. My essence comes in divine perfection to each of you; to your hearts, to your minds, to your souls, to your sweet personalities; to who you are.

"My Blue Diamond is accompanied now by the perfection of the Golden Flame essence of Yahweh and the Pink Diamond essence of your divinity. When you ignite all three flames, dear heart, it creates the integrated heart.

"The integrated heart is the balanced heart, it is the heart of clarity, patience and prudence; it is the heart of grace and generosity; it is the heart of knowing and wisdom vision. It is the heart that tells you when to go and when to stay; it is the heart that always tells you 'it is time to Love.'

"You were not born in a vacuum; you were born of our essence, among our most magnificent of creations. You are unique and it is that uniqueness that we wish to preserve and to unify. That is the purpose of the gift of the Pink Diamond. This is the gift of your own wholeness, your own sweet self, and beauty. It is not simply a matter for recognition, child, it is a matter of embracing. It is a matter of bringing in, cherishing, nurturing and allowing that blossoming, that rose to bloom. My beloved ones I ask you again to share this Pink Diamond freely with all you meet. Transmit it from your heart to theirs; transmit it to all kingdoms, all realities, and all planets. You have always been highly honed transmitters.

"There have been times in the past when you have turned to me and said 'Mother, I do not trust myself; Mother, I do not want to be a transmitter; Mother I do not want to trust my intuition.' But that is over, you have stepped forward into the fullness of who you are, and you are magnificent. So I fill your heart with Pink Diamond because while I wish always to hold, nurture and protect you, my greater desire is for you to stand in your freedom and in your expression, your divinity.

"The Golden Flame of Father burns brightly within. Your Father has told you the Golden Flame 'is the energy of the Divine Masculine, the balancer, the flame of infinite knowledge, of infinite creation, of infinite understanding of the creation codes.

It is the Golden Flame of inspiration and my beloved ones it is the Golden Flame of action.' You are a golden torch of action and wisdom.

"When you fully activate and become the embodiment of your Tri-Flame, you become the fulfillment of your promise. Do not doubt yourself dear hearts. It is your time to go blazing across the firmaments. It is your time to light up the hearts of all those who walk the planet Earth. It is your time to ascend into the reality of whichever dimension you choose to inhabit. Do not limit yourself and do not question your innate power.

"Allow your Tri-Flame to burn brightly, allow yourself to be the embodiment of that balance. Allow yourself to reach back as shower of the way to those who still rest in the old third dimension of Earth. Lift your brothers and sisters up so that they may come to play with you in the new realm of Gaia. Lift them up that they may come to truly know their brothers and sisters of the stars. Lift them up so that they may know the truth of their promise. Lift them up because of Love."

The Gift of the Sacred Heart of Jesus

Every year at the Council of Love Gathering, there is a significant attunement and gift from the higher realms. In 2011 one of the primary gifts was from our beloved Jeshua (Jesus) of his Sacred Heart.

When Jesus first told me about this gift, I was hesitant. I grew up Catholic – and still refer to myself as culturally Catholic. Let's face it, I love Christmas and every other excuse for a holiday. But with Catholicism often comes the rigidity of control, of sin, of having to earn Love. None of those beliefs reflect the reality of One. The Gift of the Sacred Heart gift made me uncomfortable because of its reference to something that is deeply revered in the Catholic religion.

But sweet ever-patient Jeshua spoke to me, and, as always explained:

"Dear heart, why shouldn't I do this, Archangel Gabrielle

gave you her golden heart of courage and joy years ago. Often, you and I have talked about giving our hearts. Now it is my turn to bestow my Sacred Heart of Love upon all who wish to receive it. I have given my life, why not my heart? For thousands of years, actually forever, my purpose has been to instill Love within the hearts of all, on behalf of All. Did you forget the purpose of this Council is to instill Love into the hearts of all?

"You hesitate because of the Catholic terminology and autocratic practices. But this is our chance to eliminate that old paradigm of control. I give this gift freely. There is no need for penance or redemption. Love does not demand that – it reunites – or should I say desires reciprocity. The gift of the Sacred Heart is the integrated heart of Love; it is the conscious indwelling of Spirit. You have received many flames; the magenta Tri-Flame and the heart Tri-Flame. All of these gifts need to become integrated into a unified whole, just like humanity needs to become a unified whole. It is the promise of the Mother and it is the promise I made to all of you so long ago.

"The gift of the Sacred Heart marks the Shift from the old to the new of Gaia, and the new of the human collective. It marks the Shift from the ego and mental body to the anchoring in your heart – and might I say the heart of reality, which is universal Love. Sweet angels, do not shy away from the Shift. We shall and are doing this together."

And so, as the time grew near for the initial bestowing of this gift at the annual Council of Love gathering, I was ready. Thereafter, as the Sacred Heart attunement has been re-gifted all over the world by all of the participants, it has been thoroughly welcomed by all who receive it.

The following is the attunement of the Gift of the Sacred Heart of Jesus. The energy is encoded in the passages so as you listen, you will absorb the attunement. So, relax and allow.

• Listen to the "Sacred Heart of Jesus" audio file.

This has been a massive attunement filled with blessings and energy expansion beyond human comprehension. To live here on Gaia during this time of Ascension and colossal shift, in human form and consciousness with the energy of the heart of Jesus Sananda embedded within us, is unfathomable. It changes everything. It's going to take a little getting used to, so please, take that time, relax and allow. Celebrate the opening with your new expanded heart. Be grateful, be humble, and stay in awe.

Jesus does not leave us hanging but now goes on to explain what lies ahead in our next step of the Ascension process:

"So many of you have been asking me, 'Jeshua, what is going on? How do I ascend? What is the mechanism, what is the lift-off, why do I not feel differently, how come it didn't happen, how come it did?'

"My friends, it makes me laugh, not at your expense, but it reminds me of so many times when you would say 'how are we going to do this? How did you do this?' And I would turn to you and say 'I didn't really do anything. I used the Mother/Father's Love and it seemed to work. Why don't you try it because you will do this and more, far more.'

"Before we go further, I wish to share with you a vision that will help you understand, and I want you to understand. Yes, you can go on faith, but your conscious and your unconscious, your ego, your personalities, they all want to know. I get it. I want you to think, so I'm going to back up a bit and explain.

"The reality that has been open, always open, for human experience is twelve dimensions and within that twelve steps, for lack of a better word. Yes, you are in a twelve-Step program, that is correct. And that is why sometimes you have confusion with people talking about multiple dimensions. For purposes of demonstration, think of all of these layers as a tower or a spiral. So within the first, the second, the third, the fourth, there are twelve layers, that is where the one hundred forty-four keeping you up at night comes from.

"Now, think of Gaia as a globe and on this spiral with many layers she has been anchored, heart anchored, moored to the third dimension. Initially she was moored quite high in the third dimension, but as the darkness fell she was pulled downward. This globe is very big, this is for you visually to understand. So although Gaia has been anchored in the third, the top of her has often been in the fourth, some of her, what you would think of as the bottom of the globe has touched the second dimension, and sometimes the first. Her positioning is not and has not been entirely static. Do not forget my beloved ones that the first dimension is home of ideas, no form. It is a wonderful, wonderful place to be but it is without form. So that is why, even within the third dimension, you have had experiences of magic, of alchemy, of seeing the fairies all the time, the elves, the other kingdoms, the elementals.

"For years, Gaia has been working her way back up that spiral. Do you understand? I hear you inquiring, asking me, 'what do you mean Lord, third, fifth, seventh, ninth, eleventh, twelfth, Thirteenth Octave?' I hear you asking me all the time, so this is the answer.

"Gaia is rising up, she is spinning up the spiral and she is anchoring or about to re-anchor in the higher dimensions. Although we are speaking of this year, 2012, but simultaneously, let's face it, a year is a very, very short period of time. So understand she has been at it for some time. Think of it – you and I have been friends for over two thousand years. One year is nothing. But I digress. Gaia is ascending, and she is going to anchor her heart in the fifth dimension. However, as she has spun, she has also grown and expanded her field, just as each of you have. So while her heart is and will be anchored in the fifth, she is so huge that she still stretches to the seventh dimension and above, at moments brushing and intersecting with touching the eighth dimension of creation. The bottom of her being, of the globe is certainly incorporating the third so that you can have an experience of physicality, and brushing the first, the place of ideas.

"However, you need to understand that the rules of the third dimension do not apply in the higher or different dimensions. So your inspirations will not necessarily come from the 1st dimension, but rather from each other, from yourself, from your higher self, from us, from the Universe, from your star brothers and sisters. Gaia will be moored in a higher realm, and so will each of you.

"Having given you this explanation, I also want to contradict myself – and you say 'well Lord, you are always doing that, first you tell us one thing then you tell us another. Which is it?' Well it is both because we do not think of the dimensions necessarily as a hierarchy. So we are using the tower spiral as a visual, but it is not an ego arrangement.

"Many of the starseeds, in fact ninety-nine percent of the starseeds come from the ninth dimension. Currently they are in the third, they are ascending to the seventh, anchoring in the fifth and, exhibiting, manifesting and visiting in the third. For all intense and purpose, most starseeds will be found in the fifth dimension because they want to stay and be close to the heart of Gaia. They basically want to be on Earth.

"Each of you desire to see the fulfillment, the return of the plan of being in physical form and knowing of Love and Joy. Some of you have begun this transcendence with Gaia on Oct. 28, 2011 and you know it "took" because you've been sitting and chatting with me and the Universal Mother; Kuthumi and Maitreya, and we're glad to have you. Some of you have come on the recent 11:11 (Nov. 11, 2011), some of you have come on 12:12 (December12, 2011).

"I suggest to you that this or any other day is a great day to travel with me. If there is no food, I will feed you; if there is no water, I will quench your thirst; if you are cold I will warm you, I will take care of you. So you come with us to anchor in the fifth.

"Ascension is a process: think of it as moving house, and think of it as moving house and leaving where you live right now in the third dimension. You've won the lottery and you're moving to another home and it will be perfectly furnished with everything you want and need. From time to time you will be bi-locating to the third dimension. This is the best explanation I can offer. You will be reaching down into the third dimension to do your work of preparing others for this glorious event, for this gift.

"Gaia has invited you to her Ascension. That is a gift beyond imagination. Yes it is the Mother's plan but it is an amazing, tremendous gift. When I ascended, I ascended home. Yes, I took form so that people would understand, but I was not dead in the ground; I did not die. This Ascension process is also not about dying, this is about living in a beautiful new reality.

"You will create Nova Earth, because you are Nova Beings, where the Cities of Light will emerge, where your star brothers and sisters will walk with you and there will be peace and harmony, equality and freedom. Having made peace with the third dimension, you can go back to the third to help your friends out; and to invite them to come along with you. But you will live in the fifth and that is why, as you adjust to this, you may feel a little dissociative, a little schizophrenic. But dear heart, you have occupied the Universe. So have no doubt, you can do this as well."

And with the energy building, and this invitation directly from the heart of One we move into the Ascension Attunements and Meditations.

Chapter 9

The Ascension Process, The Great Awakening

As we come into the home stretch, let me back up decade or so and look at the process we have been through. We have spent at least ten years, and probably closer to fifteen, pulling in all aspects of ourselves, all facets of ourselves. You know there was a point at which about five years ago around the beginning of the Iraq War, when many of us were feeling very fragmented. And one of the reasons was that we had literally hundreds of our aspects out working on various missions, many of those with Archangel Michael.

Aspects, as mentioned earlier are comparable to duplicates of your sweet self – what some think of as parallel lives – that you have sent out into the world to undertake work or tasks in alignment with your mission and sacred contract. If you are integrated and balanced you can do that, but not indefinitely and not unknowingly. I can remember the first time the Council began taking to me about aspects it made me slightly nervous and silently I prayed that I was the host.

Beginning in earnest in 2005, Mother Mary and Archangel Michael, advised us to bring those aspects back into ourselves. We then spent time integrating and calling back all facets of our beings, all our duplicates as it were, and asking them of course, before they'd come into ourselves to please wipe their feet at the door. So that process of integration took place.

That was followed shortly thereafter by a complete re-gridding, as we anchored the fullness of our soul design. Now, concurrent with that we were also receiving the gifts of the Violet Flame, the gifts of Mother Mary's Blue Diamond and then the Pink Diamond of our unique individual wholeness and divinity, the alignment of our totality and our wholeness within us. The impact of this gift of the Pink Diamond was the alignment of our higher self, our angelic self, and our I AM presence with our current personality, ego self.

Take a moment and visualize yourself in alignment with the I AM presence, with the God Source Presence. See or feel the beam of Light coming down from the Heart of One into your crown anchoring everything in your heart. Feel that same Light beam continuing down through you into Gaia, aligning with her and her purpose as well.

Every time you meditate of either going to the Thirteenth Octave or the Shift, what the Council calls the fifth dimensional meditation, it brings you into that alignment. What occurs is the Council of Love lifts us into the Thirteenth Octave, and then allows us to float very, very gently back down into the fifth or the seventh as the case may be. Many people for a long time have just been feeling themselves in the seventh. You can't do this if you aren't in alignment with your higher self and God.

On a physical level, some of you may experience poor health, upset stomach, emotional upset, disjointedness. And I'm sure you're saying to yourself 'I'm sure I didn't agree to this. Why am I experiencing lack, limitation because those are things that would be of the old paradigms of the third dimension?' It is because, at some level in the bigger plan, and your place within the bigger plan, you either have agreed to it or there is something in you that begs for surrender.

Continue to cut those cords that are now as mushy as overcooked spaghetti, and do not judge it. You are releasing something that is right at the surface, like a leaf floating on a pond. It's right at the surface to just be picked up and let go of, because if it doesn't feel like Love then it doesn't belong. And if you are reading this and saying "but I've tried and tried and nothing works. I'm really sick and tired of it." Congratulate yourself, and remember the Council has talked to us time and again about getting to the point where we are so sick and tired of something that we literally let go of it. We have reached the point of surrender because we're just so darn fed up with carrying that debris.

Surrender and letting go is not about abandoning or running away from the third dimension, it never has been. You cannot become trans-dimensional by trying to escape from the third. As we ascend you have to make peace with the third dimension. What I have discovered, is that also means making peace with all the physical aspects of the third, the most prevalent of which are things to do with our physical bodies and our physical selves. We release through meditation and visualizing whatever is plaguing you.

For example, one of my big challenges over the years has been asthma. So I visualize the asthma as standing outside of myself. I usually visualize that asthma as the twelve-year-old girl who got whooping cough, because that's where it started for me. I take her and I bring her into my heart and I hold her; I love her; I love the coughing, I love the asthma until it just dissolves into my heart like the sparkles of Pink Diamond or Blue Diamond, or my own ray of blue.

Some of our healing and clearing practices are changing as we enter this Ascension process. Before, we would often release and allow the issue to wash away as if you were standing underneath Niagara Falls. Now, we are guided to bring it into ourselves, keep it in your heart and love it into submission because somewhere in the plan, whether we like it or not, we have an agreement to do so.

If you say "well if I agreed to that I want to change my contract." Changing your soul contract is a very, very rare thing, even rarer than walk-ins. But if that's the case, you can amend your soul contract. I am not referring to situations where you are simply fed-up and ticked off and we say "that's it, I've had it." Amending your soul contract is a very sacred and, in my opinion, risky undertaking.

How you go about amending or re-negotiating your soul contract is through deep meditation and prayer. It can be done over the course of about a week. Light your candles, incense, or sage, and create your sacred space, and simply ask. My understanding of re-negotiating soul contracts is based on what I've channeled and witnessed and that's limited because it is so rare. What I've seen is often during that process, the understanding of the bigger picture of why you promised to do something or other becomes clear and the person says "oh, OK, I'll stick with it."

However, if you don't choose to stick with it, then that's how it's done. It's done through prayer and conversation with your guides, with the Father/Mother/One. It doesn't mean you have to change your whole contract; you might change one clause of it. But it's not something that's done lightly, or often.

It's important to realize however that as we Shift and anchor firmly in the fifth and the seventh dimensions that there's no physical illness; that issues which can feel so overwhelming at times, simply don't exist in the other dimensions. The key is going to the fifth or the seventh and staying there every single day. Making sure you're not getting dragged back down into the third by being attached to human drama of any description. The sensation you are seeking is head in the Thirteenth Octave, heart in the seventh dimension (or fifth), feet planted deep in the heart of Gaia.

The sense is, because you've gone through this transition, this inter-dimensional doorway, you're reaching into the third to do your work, to do whatever, but you're not grounded in the third. You don't want to go back there, that part of your contract is over and done with.

As we prepare for the Ascension meditation and attunement, read the insights offered by Jesus Sananda on what to expect.

"Greetings I am Jesus Sananda and I welcome all of you upon this beloved planet. I welcome you to this time of unity, of connectedness and balance; I welcome you home. I welcome you home not only to the fifth dimension but the seventh, if you choose. I welcome you home to my heart.

"I wish to tell you and to speak to your hearts about this upcoming year of 2012. I can hear many of you saying to me 'Lord, please whatever you say don't tell us that this chaos and turmoil will continue.' Shall I remain silent? Shall I not tell you the truth? That is not possible for me. So let me speak to you my beloved friends, this is it; this is the time when our beloved sweet Gaia ascends on her journey homeward. She spirals up into the heart of One and down into the fifth dimension, which is exactly what we will do with you today.

"It is miraculous and it is also the fulfillment of the promise made between us, particularly the Mother, the divine feminine, when Gaia volunteered to do this. It is her sacred journey, and for millions and millions and millions of years she has nurtured you; she has held you; she has taken care of you, even when there were times when she shrugged or adjusted. But with the work of all of you and yes, us, the work of your star brothers and sisters, and planetary assistance, which you have never thought of, for there are other planets also, sentient beings that are assisting Gaia in this undertaking, you know.

"Gaia wants you to be with her in this sacred journey, in this journey of Oneness, of Love. When I say 'you' I mean all of you, the trees, the water, the mountains, the air, the oceans, the birds, the snakes, the spiders, and each of you my beloved friends. She invites you all to come along. Each of you, before you came to this planet and during this reincarnation, has said 'yes, I wish to do this. I have waited so darn long for the return of Love, for the fulfillment of the plan on Earth. I am going. Nothing will stop me.' You have turned to me and you have pledged and you have said to me 'Jeshua, this time we will complete the journey of Love; we will anchor this journey within our hearts. And when the time is right and the activation occurs, we will be ready.' You are more than ready my beloved ones. Although you do not see me yet in form, I am with you – as are the Archangels, my blessed Mother, Yahweh, the Ascended Masters, the Company of Heaven, and the Legions of Light. We are in this together. So you say to me 'Jeshua, Jesus Sananda, what does this look like? What does this unfoldment look like?'

"I speak to you in global terms and while I do so, I also embed within your heart what your individual journey looks like. There will continue to be what looks like elimination or dislocation of some of the institutions, practices, environments, and ways of doing business that are not of Love. This has not changed.

"There is a place for commerce, for the exchange of what you create and trade, that is not a problem. There is a place for those who wish to engage in politics, but it is politics that are based on the thirteen Blessings and Virtues. It is societies that are based fundamentally on Love, that do not include the paradigms of old Earth, of greed, of lust. We do not even want to talk about it. So that will be fading away but at the same time things will be coming on. The new is already emerging; you see it all around you. Sometimes you go like this, then you are afraid to look and afraid to hope just in case it isn't real because you do not want to be duped or disappointed. Turn and face it because this is your time and your creation with Gaia.

"The Light grows, the energy you hold; your crystalline body, all of this is coming on line. It is already well, well underway. New institutions, new understandings of what this means will also emerge, and that is important. You do not arrive in the fifth dimension as if you are going to a resort, a Club Med, or Club Galilee; it is not an all-inclusive service. But it will feel that way because the ability to create, to manifest, to build what you wish to build is simple because the illusions and the density of the third dimension is gone. It is already over. It is an illusion that is disintegrating.

"The lesson is to let it go and to embrace the wholeness of your being, to embrace the wholeness of your community, and dear hearts, your community is the human collective and everything else that is upon Earth. It is necessary during this time of transition that you also make peace with the third dimension. And you say, 'well what do you mean, how do I do that?' You do it by blessing everything you have known in that reality. It is not merely what you perceive as the physicality. What you have thought of as the third dimension, as duality, polarity, all of that is gone. It simply will not exist. If you really wish to continue in that struggle then we will take you elsewhere; you will not be harmed or die, but you will be taken elsewhere.

"My Mother's plan is to invite each and every one of you on this journey, because dear hearts, it is exciting. It is playful, it is fun, it is not drudgery; it isn't something you are working at. Remember when we sat together and laughed, and played, and broke bread and created bread, that is what this journey is about, and we invite you.

"Do not attach and do not judge, for we know the trouble that can cause. Do not judge what you see dissolving, disintegrating, and whatever you do, don't judge your fellow human beings. Each and every one of them are bright angels on a mission. This is a time of co-creation like never before. We have done a great deal of co-creation, as have your star brothers and sisters, but it has always been in the reality that you were occupying.

"The rules change as you shift dimensions. One of the wondrous qualities of the fifth dimension is the ability to manage change, to bring forth change, and your societies; your planet is more than ready. You have seen the forerunners of this. There is resistance in some sectors. The key to this is to send them Love, send them Michael's Blue Flame of Truth, and send them my Sacred Heart. Send them the magenta, send them the Blue Diamond of the Mother, but send to them and bless them and help them to understand the world has changed, and it has changed for the better.

"You have been preparing for this with me for for thousands of years. You have walked with me and you have sat with me and you have broken bread with me and we have talked of these things before, my friends. Often you have turned to me and you have said 'Jeshua, won't it be wonderful when everyone in the village and everyone in the town understand that this is the time of Love.' This is the lesson, the teaching, and the gift that you carry. I would turn to you and say to you 'What makes you think it's just me carrying it? I did not come to walk alone. I did not come to be in the desert – only now and then when I needed to struggle with my own demons and didn't wish to burden you.'

"My friends, we do this together. And what do I mean by 'this,' this discussion of Ascension, Decension, Shift? I use the word of Ascension because it is a word and an understanding that each of us have talked about before; it is the shifting of realities, it is that inter-dimensional Shift, and it is with the taking and the presence of your physical form. If you wish to ascend without your body then you talking about a very different experience of what you think of as death or transition. That was not why I called this party. There will be no hasty departures from this undertaking.

"It is the raising up of vibration which you have already been doing and my dear hearts, you have been doing it for years. You have been penetrated by the raising again of the frequencies in the last year, really in the past twenty-five years, but there has been an increasing intensity which now is month to month. It is by the holding of that vibration of Love that you simply get lift-off. Yes, you are assisted by many above and below.

"This is not about leaving your loved ones behind; it is not about pain and sorrow. It is not about abandoning those you care about. I know, I had to do that. We will not revisit that ever again for it was far too hard. It is about accessing and anchoring your inter-dimensional self. It is about traversing from the fourth, to the fifth, to the sixth, to the seventh, and when you arrive in the seventh I will be there waiting for you, and I will also be waiting for you in the fifth and the third. It is a time of transformation and the transformation is the understanding and the anchoring of the Mother's Plan of Love.

"You are seeing the decay, the breaking down, what some would call destruction, of the paradigms that have not served. When there is Love there is no room for greed, hatred, bigotry, or limitation. Let me be clear with you – you have never, ever been limited; you just thought you were. Let it go, let it all go. You have been called. We have beckoned to you as the pathfinders, the keepers of Gaia, the bridges to the star brothers and sisters, the healers, the channels, the teachers, this doesn't change. Only now we add the gate-keeper role because, you go through this portal again and hold the door open for those to follow you. This process of Ascension is just that, it is a process, and it is a process that has lasted a long time. If you think you are ready, and you have been fed-up, we are more than ready. So we join with you, all of us join with you.

"The heart decision has always been yours. It was yours ten thousand years ago, and it is yours now. I already know your heart says 'yes.' Last year, I spoke to you about claiming your freedom; of stepping forward into the reality of who you are, of anchoring your Pink Diamond wholeness, of expanding the truth, and you have done so. Yes, sometimes kicking and screaming, sometimes laughing and playing. I would suggest the laughing and playing, it's far more delightful. Ascension is to be in the center of your being, in the center of your being. It is not just to Love, it is to be the Love, and you are.

"So many of you say 'Jeshua, what lies ahead?'

"On Earth there are many words that are overused. So if I say to you 'remarkable, incredible, magnificent transformation', you go 'yeah OK, I know that'. And what does it look like? Gaia is spinning faster than ever. She has begun and what you have done is not only for yourself but a deep reassurance to her. You have expressions that you are ready for lift-off; well she is ready for take-off. You have done the preparation, you have made the flight. So you reassure not only the human collective, reassure Gaia that she does not need to do any further shrugging; she does not need to give, shall we say, strong messages to get ready. Gaia has no desire to create devastation, cleansing yes, devastation no.

"It is not about oceans overtaking land mass. There has been drift of the axis of about three degrees over the past thirty years, which some of you have noted as changing weather patterns. The Shift goes south by southwest, and is very marginal. A pole shift will not take place. There will not be extended periods of darkness. The electrical grids will be recharged. You will have visitations with your star brothers and sisters, and the availability of new technology.

"This Shift is about unity; this is about what we talked about, what we came together for thousands of years ago. It was to build a community of Love. St. Germaine, my dear friend and physician, used to tease you and call you "M and M's," masters-in-the-making. Now you are simply in your mastery. The only thing that bars you from this is your own sense of self-acceptance. We are pleased there is enough ego to accept it. Do not deny who you are for it belittles us.

"Now it is important as you go about your work to be completely in balance. This balance issue is one of concern, for you can no longer have a person or a planet out of balance. That is not the plan. Take time for your sacred self; take time to listen, to create, and to be who you are. Yes the changes are rapid and your physical form will become stronger and stronger. But that does not mean that we are asking you to be tri-athletes. We are asking you to be in the balance; that means rest, play, staring at the wall and honoring what you need. Not next week, not when you can fit it in and that doesn't just go for the rest. It doesn't work that way, time is now. You have entered a dimensional reality where time is very different my friends. So I would suggest you adjust your watches, or toss them, unless you like the jewelry. Go with my Love."

We are being given such remarkable visions and understanding of what lies ahead, and what the Shift entails. Never to be outdone, Universal Mother Mary also wants you to have a glimpse of the gifts of Love and joy in form that are in store as you enter the higher dimensions.

"Greetings. I am Mary, and so I continue, and I say continue because dear heart we have been having this conversation for eons. When I say to you that I am the Mother of All, I want you to take it very personally. I am not some distant deity, some entity that floats on clouds and decides whether to grant you joy or not. Joy was built into the Love, dear hearts, and it is part and parcel of every particle, every molecule, and it is who you are. You tend to drift in and out of joy and when you drift away what you do, whether it is consciously or unconsciously, is you choose to put yourself in a place of disconnection. And not only disconnection to me, to all the beings above and below, but disconnection to yourself, and disconnection to your ability to bring forth what your heart truly desires.

"We have given you many tools, the most precious being the Gift of the Thirteenth Octave, the gift of Divine Union that gives you the connection above the twelve realms, dimensions and twelve planes within each of those dimensions of your reality. It is the embodiment of your spirit in union with us, and with that has come a plethora of gifts, of teachings, of tools, so many that you forget and that does not matter, we never take offense. For the point is to have luxurious choices, because choice and free will is also the gift of this planet. It was to know Love and joy in form.

"Now you have worked diligently, destroying the old belief systems created by the humans. You are seeing the truth of your existence and you are ready to let go, and fly free. The foundation of blessings, virtues, connection, flames, and diamonds, is to assist you in flying free; in creating your future reality. You do not simply arrive in fifth or sixth or seventh dimension and everything is completed awaiting your arrival. No, part of what you are doing is co-creating what the forms will look like. No, you are not arriving to a desert, but even the desert is very rich. But the choices of creation are yours.

"The embodiment of energy into form is the next adventure. And the embodiment of Love into form is the fulfillment of my plan, and dear hearts, it is the fulfillment of your plan. It is the only reason you have reincarnated at this time. I have heard your cries and sometimes your pleas in the dark of night saying 'what on Earth am I doing here?' You are here as anchors, as beacons, as showers of the way, but you are also on Gaia to have this experience of explosion/implosion and forward movement in unity and in Love.

"This situation is called the Shift, the Great Awakening. It is the term that we have used with this channel for a very long time because it connotes the Shift and Awakening not just one part of your being, but in the collective, in the planet, in the kingdoms, in the multiverse. This is all about you as beautiful, unique, individual soul, and, it is all about everything. You are unified, you are part of a unified grid, you always have been, and you always will be. That is a gift. So acknowledge it. Do not sit in solitary. Rather, turn to those around you, both in your community, your soul family and spiritual community. Unite. We have taught you the very simplest formula of co-creation, and frankly we are astounded you do not use it more. And we have said to you many times 'the game changed dear ones; we are in sacred partnership.' I do not instruct my legions of angels to do to you, occasionally for you, but the message of the day is with you.

"Many of you are very anxious and yearning for the change, for the Shift, for the arrival of your star brothers and sisters, for the visibility of your Cities of Light, for your crystal temples, for the healing of humanity, but take time to create because you are part of that Shift with us. We cannot do this to or for you. You are working on the healing and creation of leaderships that allow disclosure and movement and the creation of different financial realms and ways of doing things that are based on access and co-creation rather than limitation. You have put in positions of power and leadership and trust, those who understand what their mission and purpose is. "What I am asking is for you to help. Are we underway? Absolutely. Seldom do we speak of what you think of in your realm as timelines. But let me suggest that the time is short.

"I invite you to receive the attunement and energy transference that will lift you gently and gracefully into the fifth or seventh dimension. Allow yourself an hour for this precious gift from the heart of One."

• Listen to the "Ascension" audio at this point.

Chapter 10

Looking into the Future

There are many unknowns in this incredible journey we are taking together. Archangel Michael tells me more than thirty million people have made, or are in the process of making, the Ascension transition. But collectively we still don't know the fullness and details of everything that lies ahead. But we do know that it will be better, filled with miracles, creation and Love. I for one can't wait.

We live in an incredible time within this Universe and upon Gaia. The Council has told us of other planets that have evolved and ascended – Venus, Halion and Tralana. But it has never happened here on Earth, it has never happened within any of our human lifetimes. If ever there was a time for hope this is it. When I think of looking forward this is the quality that sticks out above everything else. We are living in an incredible time of hope.

Universal Mother Mary has often told us, "if there is no hope there is no life." I couldn't agree more – and I would add if there is no hope there is no fun, no excitement. Trust and hope are inexorable twins, and I get caught in the chicken and egg debate when I try to separate them. Never have we as the human collective lived when the qualities and virtues of hope and trust are so vitally necessary. If we don't merely hold the vision but proceed, each of us, to unfold the vision then we will miss an unparalleled opportunity.

Think of it; there are beings from all over the galaxies and far beyond who have come to witness, help and participate in this Great Awakening. Ascended Masters, Archangels, the Legions of

Light and the Company of Heaven reach out to us and invite us to be in partnership, to co-create this miraculous goal of the human collective ascending with Gaia. The opportunity is not for Gaia to ascend – that's a done deal. The opportunity, the gift, is for us to go with her. The offer, the Plan, is for us to be conscious trans-dimensional beings, while in form. My imagination goes wild exploring the possibilities of what it will be like. And then I realize I have no idea. My third dimension mind and experience is too limited. And so, I cycle back to hope. Hope tinged and bursting with excitement, anticipation and wonder.

I thought in closing the New Year's message from the Universal Mother on the themes and what lies ahead in 2012 would be a perfect conclusion.

"Greetings, I AM Mary, Universal Mother, Mother of Love, Mother of change, Mother of the omniverse, Mother of One, and Mother, sweet angels, of each of you. My beloved children, I welcome you home to my heart, but also home to Earth to this beloved planet that I have birthed; home to the place as it was intended, as the restoration continues. Do not underestimate how much has been accomplished and how much has been done. There is far more that has been completed than remaining.

"This does not mean the creation will stop or there will not be further expansion, for that would be ridiculous, and each of you, including us, would be extremely bored for we are always in creation; it is infinite and constant. This is something I wish you to truly incorporate and understand into the very core of your being. Sometimes you turn to me and you say 'Mother why has this or that not happened?' I am always anxious, eager and happy to respond to you. Part of that answer is for you to look at what your participation in the daily creation as well. You are mature souls. In fact you are some of the oldest souls throughout the Universe. It is not that you do not have the wisdom to understand because you do, you always have.

"I did not come this day to talk about self-fulfilling prophesies. I came to tell you and, to engage you with my Love, and to share from our perspective what the themes are for the upcoming times.

"What you need, dear heart is patience and prudence, passion and action. Yes, it runs the full gamut. Let me explain. Many of you are frustrated at times because what you see in front of you does not appear to be moving quickly enough for your liking. We certainly understand that, because very often it does not move quickly enough for our liking either. But never do we interfere to such an extent as to override human action or human will because that is part of the entire plan and the transition. It is the partnership we are in, we do this together, angels above and angels below.

"What you are doing is practicing patience and prudence. When I say prudence I don't mean sitting around and waiting patiently. I mean to put yourself prudently where you belong. You say to me 'Mother, what do you mean?' This is a time of chaos and unfoldment; simultaneous to a time of miracles, new realities and beginnings. There are also those who are kicking and screaming as the old falls away and the new is reborn, and I don't want you in that line of fire. Do not put yourself in that position unless that is your role. Let me reassure you it is a role very few of you have.

"So be prudent in your choices of what you choose to do and where you choose to place your energy, who you choose to be with; how you choose to spend your time, and your energy. Prudence has always been thought of as rather boring but it is really not, for it is the ultimate discernment. It is knowing the ramifications and the inner workings, the outcomes of any choice and decision. So I ask you during this time of change, during this time of Ascension, be very prudent.

"Most of you are already on your way to the fifth, and then through to the seventh dimension. And of course, you are reaching back and you are acting as guides, as friends, as helpers for those remaining in the third reality. You are helping them through the doorway. Be prudent where you position yourself as you reach back into the third and make sure you are not being pulled back into the third. It is not where you belong and it is not where you work most effectively. It is no longer your place of joy.

"You cannot do this Ascension work until you have made peace with the third. This is not an escape plan. This is making peace with the beauty of the third dimension, with everything it has to offer, of embracing it, thanking it, patiently letting go and then moving forward. And as you move forward we want you, we ask you, we encourage you, to be absolutely in your passion. Yes this incorporates Love, Light, joy, and enthusiasm. Do and be your passion.

"We have talked a lot about taking action, meaningful action, prudent action, and you say to me 'Mother, what do you mean by this and how do I know which action I should take? There are so many choices in this wonderful, diverse Gaia.' What I ask of you is to take the actions you are passionate about, that excite you, turn your fire up, make you smile and laugh, and excited to be alive. This is not about dying, this is not about leaving. This is about living as you were intended, angels in form, having the joy of physicality, knowing Love in physicality.

"If you are not passionate about what you are doing, then I would ask you 'What are you doing and why are you wasting your time doing it?' Do not tell me 'it is because I have to pay the rent Mother.' That is an old excuse and it is of the old paradigm. You are mighty creators. You are in partnership not only with us, with the entire Council, with Sanat Kumara, with Yahweh; you have been given the keys to the Warehouse of Heaven. I'm not saying there are not moments or days when you feel sad, when there are situations that make you unhappy. But by and large, if you are living your passion, if you are taking actions according to the passion of your heart, then you are living your journey and your life.

"This passion and joy is essential not only for your Ascension but for the Ascension of the collective. It is throwing away, erasing, eliminating, using Archangel Michael's sword and shield. The Violet Flame is also handy to eliminate what you think or believe or know does not work in your life, because you are not bringing that forward. Be prudent about what you are packing and what you are taking along on this next adventure. Be reassured, in the higher dimensions there is no room for death, destruction, disease, lack or limitation. You cannot apply what you have known as the rules of the third reality, of the third dimension, to any other dimension because it has been sullied by the human construct of illusion and what we call delusion.

"These are the watch words for the coming year: patience, prudence, passion and action. If you do not know, if you are not sure which way to turn, turn directly to me, I will help you. That is my greatest joy; that is my passion. I am prudent not to interfere, but the unfoldment of the plan is at hand. When we say to be patient, we do not mean to be inert. It is to be wise and observing of what is transpiring around you and not to move precipitously, to not go to anger or frustration precipitously. You are assisted like never before. So action means just that; it does not mean staying in your cave, in your home, in your sacred space all the time. You must mingle amongst people, and take the risk to express what you know to be true, to share the light in your way, not in mine, but also in ways that are prudent enough that people hear you.

"We have enormous faith, confidence, trust, belief in you. That is why we are in partnership, forever. Let us proceed with great joy and passion. Continue the work you do with our beloved Archangel Michael, continue your collective work of meditation and healing, they are having profound effect. Continue to work with individuals in the financial or political arenas. Continue to send the messages of connection to your star brothers and sisters; continue to visit them on board ship. Continue bravely and courageously and know that we are with you, all of my legions; all of my realms are with you. Go in peace and go with my Love. Farewell."

How do you finish a book about such a radical transformation as Ascension, of a whole planet waking up and remembering? What is left to be said after we have gone through the Thirteenth Octave, been imbedded with the thirteen Blessings and Virtues, received the Violet and Tri-Flame Flame initiations, been gifted with the essence of the Mother and Father, and come to know the divinity of our sweet selves?

The steps we have walked through together are not just a possible or suggested method of Awakening. They are sure-fired, tried and true energetic catalysts to assist you, your family, your friends and the Lightholder community to get where we are going. Do the meditations, read the words, and receive the energetic attunements again and again until they are absolutely anchored in the core of you. Keep doing this until your head is in the Thirteenth Octave, your heart in the fifth dimension and your feet planted firmly in the heart of Gaia. We're all depending on you, and you are depending on each and every Lightholder on the planet. This is the heart and soul of unity and community and we are doing it together.

Don't forget there are millions already in the process; there is a group of us who have already done this and we are holding the door open for you. We are waiting for you. We are holding out our hands to help you through that portal, and we can't wait to see you.

It is important to be gentle with yourself and remember Ascension is a process. Awakening is a process, and each of us is uniquely different how we do this. The process outlined ,by the Council of Love will hold and lead you through this cycle of human evolution. The entire company of Heaven, the Council of Love and your dearly beloved guides are right here to help you. If ever there was a time to ask for help, to step forward in co-creation, it's now. Your job is trust, action, allowing and Love. After all, Love is all there is. Love is All.

Ascension is not the Big Bang on December 21, 2012, or any other particular date for that matter. Ascension is the Great Awakening. Your slumber is over. It is time to rise and shine. Then it is time to gently and compassionately awaken everyone around you, so that we may fly as One with Gaia. I look forward to hearing from you about your journey – about the miracles and openings you are experiencing. Thank you from the bottom of my heart for joining me in our Ascension. See you in the fifth dimension.

About the Audio Files

There are four audio files that come with this book:
1. The Thirteenth Octave
2. Temple of the Violet Flame
3. Sacred Heart of Jesus
4. Ascension

E-Junkie

The audio files accompanying this book are accessible depending on which format you are reading this book. If you purchased the book through e-Junkie, the files are attached as separate MP3 files.

Kindle

If you purchased this book through Amazon.com as a Kindle book, go to http://www.e-junkie.com/counciloflove. There you will see a listing for The Great Awakening Audio Meditations. Purchase the downloadable file and enter this code **13Love** for a 100% discount.

E-reader

If you purchased this book for a different e-reader, go to http://www.e-junkie.com/counciloflove. There you will see a listing for The Great Awakening Audio Meditations. Purchase the downloadable file and enter this code **13Love** for a 100% discount.

Hard copy/Amazon

If you purchased this book as a physical copy, go to http://www.e-junkie.com/counciloflove. There you will see a listing for The Great Awakening Audio Meditations. Purchase the downloadable file and enter this code **13Love** for a 100% discount.

For help, contact admin@counciloflove.com,

About the Author

Linda Dillon had been the channel for the Council of Love (COL, or the Council) since 1984 after a near-death experience from a car accident opened her heart to her true purpose.

As the vehicle for the Council, Linda channels the vibration of pure Love into the hearts of those who come to her. These people are always recognizable by the dramatic personal changes and transformation they are going through. Channelings are for the transmissions of universal information, as well as to assist people to connect and work with their own personal guides.

Linda channels Jesus Sananda, Mother Mary and Yahweh, as well as the ascended masters such as St. Germaine, Sanat Kumura, and Maitreya, the Apostles and the Archangels, Gabriel, Michael, Raphael, Uriel and Jophiel. While the energies and personalities of each being are unique, the vibration of Love, pure and simple remains consistent.

Having had a successful career as a health care executive, Linda understand the need to make spiritual matters hands-on and practical. She teaches workshops and webinars throughout the year and has a worldwide client base who request individual channelings. She is the CEO of the Council of Love, Inc., and the Nova School of Healing Arts and Sciences, an approved Florida Continuing Education provider in energy healing.

Linda resides on the Treasure Coast of Florida and can be reached through her website, www.counciloflove.com.